For
Your message
matters!

ONLINE SALES FORMULA

ONLINE SALES FORMULA

A PROVEN SIX STEP MODEL
TO INCREASE YOUR IMPACT AND INCOME ONLINE

Dr. Brian J. Dixon

TABLE OF CONTENTS

Introduction   1
   Write your own your manifesto   2
   Defining who you serve (exercise):   2
   Your ideal customer avatar   3
      The best way to define your ideal customer avatar   4
      Parker, the sales trainer   4
      Nicole, the realtor   4
      Introducing the Barefoot Football Player   6
   Don't do this alone   7
   Getting clear on your why   7
   Consistent effort in the same direction over time   7
   Three numbers to measure   8
      Visitors   8
      Subscribers   8
      Customers   8

Do you know your numbers?	9
A system for knowing and growing your numbers	10
First impression	10
Lead magnet	10
Opt-in page	10
First Impression	**11**
Creating the first impression	12
Domain Names	16
Attracting Website Traffic	18
How do you actually get people to your website?	18
Two Ways to Get People To Your Website	19
Your Perfect Traffic Blend	19
Earned Traffic	20
Search engine rankings	20
Four additional tips	21
Referral links	22
Paid Traffic	22
Would you like a free sample?	22
A few tips on advertising online:	24
Warnings about paid traffic:	24
No clear call to action	24
Not split testing	25
Where to advertise on Social Media	25
Twitter	25
Facebook	26
Best practices for paid ads	26
Targeted audience	26
Clear Call to Action	26
Custom landing page	27
Google Adwords	27
YouTube	27

Retargeting	28
Basic guidelines for successful online advertising:	28
What about social media?	28
YouTube	30
Something else to consider about YouTube	30
Instagram	31
Following	31
Apply The 8:1 Principle	31
Use Video	31
Facebook	32
Other social networks	32
Social sharing	33
Which channels to focus on?	33
Focus on a few	33
A unified experience	34
Just like a store	34
The franchise prototype design	35
High-quality	36
Characteristics of high-quality content include:	36
References to other quality content online	36
Multimedia	36
Relevant content	37
Consistency	37
Search engine optimized	37
Improving the first impression	38
Three Quick Ways to Improve your Website	38
1. Move to a self-hosted WordPress website.	38
2. Add a lead magnets giveaway with an opt-in to your email newsletter.	38
3. Benchmark your website.	38
Benchmark your website	39

Choosing three benchmark sites	39
Reverse engineering success	40
The Anatomy of a Website	40
Above the fold	40
How a Website Works	41
The Basic Process	42
Website Hosting	44
Website Platform	44
Lead Magnet	**45**
Why you need a lead magnet?	45
So what is a lead?	46
Lead magnet tips	46
The Power of an email address	46
But I have nothing to sell	47
Types of Lead Magnets	47
Toolbox	47
A Special Preview	48
Surveys and Quizzes	49
Tips for Surveys and Quizzes	50
A Checklist	50
A Three-Video Series	52
Video 1 - the Problem	52
Video 2 - the Process	52
Video 3 - the Plan	53
Parker	53
Free mini course training	54
How to Build a Mini-Course	56
Downloadable PDF	59
What Makes a Lead Magnet Magnetic?	59
Attractive	59
Enabling	60

Want vs. Need	60
What vs. How	60

Opt-in Page — 62

Make the offer clear	63
Opt in options	63
Opting In	64
The rules of opting in	64
The tools you need for opting in	65
Requiring the minimum asking for the maximum	67
Serving all as you would serve one.	69
Where to Put it and How it Works	70
Characteristics of a great Opt-In page	71
Don't Be Cutesy	71
Keep it Clear and Simple	71
Test Your Form on Multiple Devices	72
Single Opt-In	72
One Call to Action	72
Opt-In tools	73
Sidebar opt-in boxes	73
Pop-up boxes	73
Landing pages	74
Customizing your leadpage	75
Vary the colors	75
Writing headlines	76
Improve your images	76
Advanced tip	77
How to set up your first lead page	77
Pop-up boxes	78
Delayed pop-up	78
Exit intent pop-up	78
First time only	78

Opt-in technology	79
Optimization	79
Methods to optimize your opt-in	80

Autoresponder 81
How to Use Email to Nurture Your Prospects	81
What should I say?	84
How to setup an autoresponder	84
How the system works	86
Building a relationship	86
Your autoresponder sequence	87
Example Email Zero	87
EMAIL ONE: Here is your lead magnet	88
Example Email One:	88
EMAIL TWO: A little known industry secret	89
EMAIL THREE: "A solution for you, [Name]."	91
Example Email Three	91
EMAIL FOUR: Customer testimonial	92
Example Email Four	93
EMAIL FIVE: Almost gone (last email)	94
Example Email Five:	94
EMAIL SIX: Convert to newsletter	94
So what makes a great email?	94
Solid teaching	94
Respect the inbox	95
Developing a swipe file	95
Working through the sequence	95

Teasing the Offer 96
By the way selling	96
Retargeting and Facebook pixels	98
Teasing the offer by nurturing	98

Your goal	98
Did you know?	101

Sales Page — 102
- The jargon — 102
  - Conversion rate — 102
  - A swipe file — 103
  - Minimum viable product — 103
  - Split testing — 104
- How to develop new products — 105
- When you have a truly original idea — 105
- Integrate your survey with your CRM — 106
- Video overview — 106
  - One. Text on screen — 106
- Sales video — 107
- Elements of the Sales Page — 108
  - Overview video — 111
  - Outline of the program — 114
  - Testimonials — 114
  - Features and Benefits — 114
  - Clear results — 116
  - Clear content — 116
  - Guarantee — 117
  - Clear audience — 117
  - Clear value — 117
  - Clear offer — 118
  - Call to action — 119
- How to create a sales video — 121
  - Expert tip — 121
- Video hosting options — 122
- Pricing Strategy — 123
  - Price is a secondary consideration — 124

Next Steps 125
   Best Practices 125
Relaunching 126
   Launching a re-engagement campaign 126
   How do you reengage your list? 128
   Your monthly marketing plan 129
Using business intelligence 130

Advanced Techniques 131
   Website Analytics 131
   Autoresponders based on user behavior 132
   Abandoned Cart 132
   Retargeting 132
      Introducing Retargeting 133
   Sequences and Tags 135
      Low-priced, mid-priced, and high-priced. 138

Bonuses 139
   Three email sequence to sell self-study course 139
      Email 1: Introducing the Opportunity 140
      Email 2: Social Proof and Momentum 140
      Email 3: Straight Sale 141
   14 Income Channels 142
Let's connect 142

INTRODUCTION

You have a message to share and an audience to serve. You have something unique to contribute to the marketplace, and you should be paid well for that contribution. You can engage your "thousand true fans" and make a very generous income by providing service to others. Online sales do not need to be sleazy, pushy, cheesy, or scams. Instead you can engage a niche tribe by creating valuable content that serves your audience and nurtures them into becoming your ideal customers.

That is the manifesto of this book, and believing in it is essential. It is the foundation of everything we're about to cover. As we get started on our journey together, it would be worth it for you to take a few minutes to complete the following exercise before we talk about online sales formulas and I walk you through my six step floats model.

Write your own your manifesto

The following example expresses the core concepts that your manifesto should: "I have a message to share and an audience to serve. I have something unique to contribute to the marketplace and I should be paid well for the contribution."

In my work with content creators (authors, speakers, bloggers, and small business owners), I have found that the most successful are crystal-clear on the message they communicate and the audience they serve. The ones who struggle the most and have the biggest challenge engaging an audience and making a living online, are unclear on both their message and their audience.

So, before I teach you the system I use on a daily basis with my clients at the Dixon Agency, it would be worthwhile for you to formulate a clear message and define your target audience.

Defining who you serve (exercise):

Take a minute and study this exercise I stole from my friend and client Dan Miller (48days.com):

"I help _____ do _____ so that they can _____."

For example:

"I help authors grow their businesses online so they can increase their impact and income."

"I help stay-at-home moms organize learning activities for their children so they can find peace in the midst of a hectic day."

"I help retired military personnel reenter the workforce by taking them through a four week training program so they are able to find work that they love."

Okay, now it's your turn to fill in the blanks.
I help _____ do _____ so they can _____.

In order to move on, you should be able to complete the following exercise:
My name is _____.

I hope _____ will do _____ so that they can _____.

I do this through _____ on _____.

My ten-year vision is to _____.

My three-year vision is to _____.

My one-year vision is to _____.

Next week, I need to _____.

Note: If it's difficult for you to complete this exercise for yourself, try completing it for someone you respect in your industry.

Your ideal customer avatar

As you launch or relaunch your online funnel, you should focus on one person.

This person is your dream client. Marie Forleo calls this person your ideal customer avatar (ICA). The more you know him/her, the better you can serve him/her. With each of my clients we go through an ideal customer avatar exercise where we give the ICA a name. All of the emails that we write, all of the sales copy that we use, even the way that we price products and programs are all filtered through the lens of that ICA.

The best way to define your ideal customer avatar

Instead of going through a complicated process to create an ideal person, the best way to define your ideal customer avatar is to actually pick one. Choose one real person that you have a relationship with that you can actually talk to. Take the time to sit down with this person and get to know their compelling needs, wants, and goals. Consider ways that your products and programs could benefit this person.

Feel free to ask open ended questions about pricing, format and file type, and other aspects of your business. By talking to real customers I have helped my clients improve the pricing of their programs, increase email optimist by changing the content of their lead magnet, and adjusted the design of the website to better suit the customers needs given the fact that they used their iPhone to access the website much more frequently than their desktop computer. You may be surprised at the kinds of information you'll glean by talking to a real person that you are trying to serve online.

Here are two examples of this exercise:

Parker, the sales trainer

Hello, my name is Parker. I help commission-based sales representatives develop a sales routine so they can make more sales and have a clear strategy that they do not need to continually reinvent. I do this by sharing an inspirational blog post on my blog, interviewing sales experts on my weekly podcast, and providing sales training through my online coaching programs.

Nicole, the realtor

Hi, my name is Nicole. I help realtors in their first five years develop their brand identity in order to enable them stand out in the marketplace and increase their reputation, their referral relationships, and ultimately, their revenue. I do this through my local workshop series for realtors, my involvement in the Realtor Association, and my paid online training program.

As you can see from the first two examples, there's a clear path to revenue. Both Parker and Nicole offer a program which teaches people how to make more sales. The same could be true for entertainment or fitness. From my experience, the three easiest topics to sell are: how to make money, how to get fit, and how to achieve great relationships. People are willing to pay for these top three. However, what about more nuanced topics?

Meet **Krista**. Krista is a Christian women's blogger who shares inspirational content from the Bible to encourage stay-at-home moms to live a godly life and trust God in all circumstances.

Do you see the difference? Being a Christian women's blogger whose main goal is to encourage may make it a bit more difficult for Krista to find a clear path to revenue. Is it even possible for Krista to make money by sharing her message? Before you check out because you're not a women's Christian blogger, this exercise is applicable to you if you have any sort of inspirational message to share. In fact, most of the bloggers I speak with are just starting out and they don't see how they could ever make money from their message.

Ask yourself the following question: "Is there anyone in my niche who is making the kind of impact and income I dream about?" If there is, you can follow the general steps he/she took that lead to success. For Krista, all she needs to do is look at others in her industry who make a great living sharing their inspirational message. She can look to these writers as examples and model her business to fit her unique personality and approach.

There are other people who have gone before you and have figured this thing out. There is someone making $1 million a year sharing content that is similar to yours. As unique as you may be, there are other techniques you can learn. Don't give up your unique voice, but don't become a barefoot football player.

Introducing the Barefoot Football Player

Even if you're not a sports fan, you've likely seen a football game. Football is a rough sport. Players wear a lot of equipment and train their bodies for hours so they can crush each other. One essential piece of equipment that every football player wears, without exception, is his shoes. Not just regular shoes, but football cleats. These special shoes have padding on the toes and the heel because the player's feet are going to get stepped on by the other players. They also have cleats or small spikes on the bottom of the shoe to help the football player get a better grip while he's running with the ball, sprinting down the field, or trying to tackle the opponent.

I have watched a lot of football in my time, and besides the occasional kicker - which frankly doesn't count - I have never seen a barefoot football player. It just doesn't make any sense. It would be dangerous and it is against the rules. However, you, as a blogger, might be the equivalent of a barefoot football player.

If you want to make money and build traffic to your website, there are certain rules to follow in the online world. You will need certain equipment and you will need to understand principles that have been proven time and time again.

Can a football player technically save money by not purchasing shoes? Absolutely. Can he save time by not having his foot measured and having to go find shoes that match the uniform? Of course. You can also save some time and money, but does it make any sense? Do the benefits of saving time and money outweigh the negative impact of having your bare foot stepped on by a 300 pound football player with spiked cleats?

In the same way, there are rules about blogging; proven principles you should follow if you want to build a lasting impact. Therefore, my challenge to you is not to become the barefoot football player. Instead, follow the rules, look at the proven models, and figure out what you can learn and apply to your online business.

Now that you've found a model to follow, seek out a mentor to help guide you in your development. Do you have someone to whom you can look for guidance and insight? Someone who knows your industry? Most successful people have had someone who is already successful guiding the way. Who is that person for you?

Don't do this alone

Getting feedback and encouragement is a big part of growing your business online. It can be lonely; especially when you're in a niche that no one else whom you know understands. I recommend joining a few Facebook groups that are focused on your niche. I have found several Facebook groups in which I engage on a daily basis to get feedback, encouragement, and advice. You might also consider starting or joining a mastermind group where you meet once a week online to talk about your business and challenge each other. Even though you're a solo entrepreneur, you don't have to do this all by yourself.

Getting clear on your why

Be clear. Write your own manifesto and read it on a daily basis. It's important for you to know your commitments, the direction you're headed, and where true north is. Otherwise, you'll never find it. When you get distracted, simply use this as a filter to remind yourself of who you are and what you're trying to accomplish.

- Who do you serve?
- What do you share?
- What platforms do you focus on?

Consistent effort in the same direction over time

If you want to truly make an impact and earn an income online, you need to commit to a specific direction and stick to it. I have also fallen into the trap of chasing after the quick dollar instead of a lasting impact. This is not to say that you can't get results quickly. I have several friends who have gone from 0 to 6 figures in 6 to 9 months online. They followed a clear model consistently.

Three numbers to measure

In order to grow your business online, you need to know the following numbers:

Visitors

Visitors are the unique number of people who actually look at your website. They arrived at your site from paid or earned messages and are invited to opt in to become a subscriber.

Subscribers

These are the people who were visitors and have now become subscribers because they entered their name and email in an opt-in form on your website or on a separate opt-in page, and downloaded a lead magnet.

Customers

A third category of people with whom you interact are your customers. These are people who became subscribers, saw an offer that you made to them through email, and decided to purchase. Once they purchased your product, they became a customer and they will remain a customer for the rest of their lives.

Knowing your numbers for these three basic categories of people is much more important than knowing the numbers than the average online business person knows. If I were to ask you right now how many visitors you get on a monthly basis, how many subscribers are currently active on your main list, and how many customers you've added in the last 30 days, you should be able to tell me these numbers.

These numbers always have a weeding-out effect. For example, you might have 1,000 unique visitors per month, 100 email newsletter subscribers, and 10 customers. This means that 10% of your visitors become subscribers, and 10% of your subscribers become customers. Industry averages vary widely, but the numbers I've seen are a 6% opt-in rate and a 2% purchase rate.

So, to summarize, in order to even get one customer, you need to increase your visitors. For example, with 10,000 unique visitors per month, you will see 600 people opt-in to your list. This ultimately translates into 12 paying customers.

Do you know your numbers?

Knowing your numbers enables you to launch products and programs successfully. The better you understand your numbers, the better you understand your customers. You can measure the impact you have on people by the numbers. Unfortunately, a lot of us struggle with these basic facts, and that is why we do so terribly when it comes to marketing and sales online. We think it's all about the message and it's all about the mission, but, at the end of the day, it's about the impact and income. Both of these can be measured. If you don't know your numbers, you don't know your business.

At the time of this writing, my two favorite shows are "Shark Tank" and "The Profit." In both shows, business owners are asked two basic questions, "What are your sales?" and, "What are your profits?" These are basic financial questions about their businesses. Yet the people on the shows often cannot answer these questions. Consequently, the "sharks" eat them alive.

When you know your numbers, you will be able to make intelligent decisions to positively affect those numbers. You will know the answers to the following questions:

- Which blog post is resonating with your audience?
- Which lead magnet increased your conversion rate?
- Which module in your training program do students begin to drop off?

When you know your numbers, you can increase your sales because you can face reality, and you need to face reality in order to improve it.

A system for knowing and growing your numbers

You've waited long enough. It's time to introduce the Online Sales Formula. I've developed a six-step process to help you attract visitors, convert them to subscribers and nurture them into customers. I call this system FLOATS, which serves as an acronym to clarify exactly what you need to do online to grow your impact and income.

First impression

Start with your first impression. When someone visits your website for the first time, does it appeal to them? Is it immediately clear that your content, products, and program will help them accomplish their goals?

Lead magnet

Give away some valuable content to encourage visitors to join your email list and become subscribers.

Opt-in page

In order to make that exchange you need an opt-in page. This is the place where visitors enter their name and email to download your lead magnet.

FIRST IMPRESSION

When someone gets to your site for the first time, they have a first impression. Because there are so many other websites to visit, other things to think about, and other things to do, you can assume that the visitor to your website will only go there once. One time. You have one chance to make an impression. Just one time.

This is the greatest mindset shift for bloggers, authors, speakers, and any kind of content marketer. You have one chance to make that impression. Statistically, your website visitors are never going to come back to your site again. This is the only time that they will ever come to your website and, statistically, they will only be there for a few seconds.

This chapter focuses on that critical first impression.

In this chapter, I'll share practical steps for improving your website that will help increase the number of visitors, engage those visitors, and convert them to subscribers, which eventually leads to them becoming customers.

The first step of your online sales formula is the first impression the website visitors have of you. If you been blogging or had an online presence for any amount of time, it's easy to forget that the majority of website visitors are coming there for the first time. If you look at your Google analytics, you'll see the percentage of first-time visitors on average across your websites, it's about 50%. #rewrite Think about that for minute. Half of everyone who comes your site has never been to your site before. So a big part of your efforts on your website should be focused on introducing people to you.

Creating the first impression

No matter how someone originally learns about your product, they will eventually land on your website. This is your opportunity to win them over and, based on statistical analysis of dozens of clients, you have just a few seconds to do that. In reality, you have about five seconds to make an impression and to encourage the visitor to stay a little longer and engage.

When someone first arrives, your website should be able to answer the following questions:

- "What is this website about?"
- "Is this website for me?"
- "How can this website help me?"
- "What is my next step?"

These questions might sound basic, but you'd be surprised at how many websites I look at on a regular basis that don't answer these questions.

Take a minute to search for information. For example, let's say you're looking to accomplish something. If you are searching online, there is a reason you're searching. Suppose you were planning a family vacation. Actually, here is a real example:

Members of our family live in State College, Pennsylvania (where Penn State is located), and we were thinking about going out for New Year's Eve.

So, we typed "New Year's Eve State College" into the search engine. Now, if I were a restaurant owner, a club promoter, or a concert producer, I would seriously consider these keywords to make sure that my website showed up in the top results. At that time, I can tell you that all four websites I visited did not answer these four basic questions:

- "What is this website about?"
  The website for the restaurant should be about why the restaurant is a good fit for me.
- "What do they offer?"
- "Where are they located?"
- "When are they open?"

I would have loved to see pictures of the restaurant, pictures of the food, maybe pictures of happy customers, and I would have loved to know if there were any specials or a reservation process.

Before learning what the restaurant offers, I need to establish my answer to the first question, "Is this website for me?" Obviously if I am looking for somewhere to hang out on New Year's Eve in State College, it should be clear that the website is for a restaurant located in State College, Pennsylvania and is open on New Year's Eve. If this is not obvious (which on this occasion it was not), then I am going to leave and not come back.

"How can this website help me?"

The third question is really the most important. I need to know if this website is the best place for me to go and receive information. So it's important for you as the blogger or small business owner to consider the functionality of the website. See, in this situation, I was ready to buy. I knew the date, I knew the time, I knew the budget, and I knew the number of people in our party. All I needed was a very clear call to action and I could've purchased. I literally had my credit card in my hand ready to buy tickets, yet all of the websites I went to failed to make this call.

This brings us to our next and last question: "What is my next step?" In the first 10 seconds, it should be clear what the website owner wants the visitor to do. 9 times out of 10, this is opting in to something. You don't want to let a website visitor get to your site and then leave. You want to invite them into a deeper engagement with you. For example, the restaurant could've had the tickets available for sale and the button could have said "Purchase your New Year's Eve tickets here!" If they didn't have specific tickets/reservations available, they could've collected my information somehow. Something as simple as "Tell us about you," or "How can we help?" with a button that somebody could actually click. It could've been a live chat feature. I simply could've said, "Hey, do you have a New Year's special available?" and someone at the restaurant or even at a customer service center somewhere would have known the answer to that question.

So let's make this practical. Remember Parker, the sales trainer? Parker is building a website focused on helping commission-based sales representatives increase their sales. To answer the questions about the first impression of his website, he himself must answer the following questions:

"What is the purpose of this website?"
To help independent sales representatives increase their sales.

"Is this website for me?"
Yes, if you have something to sell.

"How can this website help me?"
This website can help you by providing you with access to both free and paid training resources to help you increase your sales.

"What is my next step?"
Add your name and email to download our free sales script to increase your sales by 20% today.

Here's another quick exercise for you. Ask yourself:

What is the purpose of my website?
Is this website for me?
How can this website help me?
What is my next step?
Who are you targeting?

One of the best decisions you can make when you're building your online business is to focus on a specific "ideal customer avatar". (Again, credit to Marie Forleo for coining the term "ICA".) Beginning with your ideal customer avatar will serve as a filter for every decision that you make about your content, your products, and even the design of your website. So take a few minutes to describe your ideal customer avatar. This should be the bull's-eye of the target.

What can I do with this website?

Make it very clear what somebody is able to accomplish with the tool that you created. Your website is a tool. It should serve a function. This function might be education, empowerment, or access. Whatever it happens to be, make sure it's clear what people can do with your product.

When you get down to it, there are really only two ways to grow your business online: Selling more to existing customers and attracting new customers to sell to. Business that are able to employ both strategies are most successful.

The following questions to consider for first impression are:

- Who are you trying to attract?
- What can you help them do?
- How do you help them do this? What is the next step they should take?

The clearer you are in your answers to these questions, the more visitors you will convert to subscribers.

Domain Names

Domain names are an important topic when it comes to promoting your business online.

The domain name that someone visits is a big part of the first impression that they have of you. Generally, I recommend that you buy your own name, such as BrianJDixon.com. However, these names often are not available, so you may have to choose a different top level domain (TLD), such as a .us or .tv. You might even buy the domain name for each of your products and programs. For example, each one of our online courses has its own domain name. Our course to teach you how to create, edit, post, and promote videos online is available at VideoBlogAcademy.com. I recommend that you buy a domain name for each of your different products and programs.

Why you should own multiple domain names

I personally own over 30 domain names. Since each domain name costs only about $10 a year, it makes sense that an entrepreneur with a lot of ideas purchase related domains whenever one of their ideas looks like a possibility worth pursuing.

The challenge is not in acquiring the right domain name. The challenge is actually using the domain names that you have. For example, it would be better for me to just create a sales page at DixonAgency.org/productname than to spend my time buying domain names that I'm never going to use. As long as you're using the domain names you buy, purchase as many as you want.

Due to the intuitive nature of Google, someone can just hear your name and a few facts about you and they can find you with a simple Google search. Therefore, your domain name does not matter as much as it used to.

That being said, there's still something powerful about being "yourname.com". As time progresses and more people create websites, there will be even more competition for these names. Consequently, if you're able to get yours, it's worth the $10 a year to maintain registration.

If your domain is already taken (that is, when you go to GoDaddy.com and search "yourname.com", it says it is not available), there is still something you can do:

How to buy your domain name from someone else

Even if your domain name is not available, don't give up. Just as you might buy a number of domain names and never use them, someone else may have purchased your domain name with no intention to actually use it. If there is a domain name that you need that belongs to someone else, here's the process I would recommend for purchasing that domain name:

1. Try visiting that domain to see if it hosts an active website. If it is actually being used, you might need to keep looking for a different domain. If it is not actively in use, search the website for contact information.
2. Visit the database www.WhoIs.net and type in the domain name. Unless they use private registration, you will be able to obtain the domain owner's name, address, email, and phone number.
3. Start with the email address and send an email from a Gmail or Yahoo email address. Don't give away any personal contact details that might indicate you have a business in that niche. From my experience, as soon as people see that you might make a business using their domain name, the price they demand goes through the roof.
4. Write a very casual email.
   Ex: "Hello. I noticed that you own domain X. Would it be possible for me to buy it from you? I noticed most domains sell for about $15. I think I could give up to $50 for this domain."
5. Try not to look desperate!
   If they don't get back to you or they want way too much money, you might have to wait it out. Think about when you might be able to revisit the issue when someone is more likely to be desperate for cash, such as before a long holiday weekend. On several occasions,

the owner of a domain name I was interested in buying has come back to me and offered to sell it at a fairly reasonable price, i.e. a few hundred dollars. The less desperate you seem, the more willing sellers are to negotiate.

6. Keep it in perspective.

It might seem like the end of the world if you can't get the domain you were hoping for. But there are multimillion dollar businesses based on a domain name that is not a standard .com. The challenge is to look at this setback as an opportunity. Remember the content matters much more than the domain name. As long as you are Googleable, your domain doesn't matter as much as you might think.

Attracting Website Traffic

How do you actually get people to your website?

After you build your website and ensure that your first impression is exactly what you want it to be for your audience, you still need to get people to come to your website. All of the bells and whistles are worthless if nobody arrives to ring them.

Driving traffic to your site can be both a mysterious concept and a very straightforward math equation. For those without traffic, it seems mysterious, and for those who have "figured it out," it's simple math. People come to your website because they know what they're going to get. That's it. They come to your website because they're expecting something and they're going to get it.

Usually, they come to your website because they are looking for that thing that you offer, and somewhere on your website, you deliver it. It's as simple as that. You have something people want it, and your website is where they can find it.

So, when we talk about driving traffic, increasing visitors, clicks, views, or hits, the conversation needs to start with, "What are you offering and does anyone want it?" An even better way to ask the question is "Who do you serve? What do they want? How can you provide it?". It really is that simple.

I'm convinced that there is no shortcut to success and there is no magic hack or tip that is going to bring a consistent stream of high-quality traffic to your website.

That one is worth repeating. There is no trick. There are only skills, strategies, and, frankly, a little luck involved. However, creating a website has a lot more to do with consistently published, high-quality content relevant to a specific audience than any new plug-in or SEO or advertising strategy. Give the people what they want and they will tell their friends.

The most successful bloggers I know were blogging before it was cool. For years (usually 4 or more), they were publishing high-quality, relevant content for a niche audience that they were a member of. I know that's probably not what you want to hear and I must confess from personal experience that the clients who have been the most frustrated are those who are looking for a quick fix. A turnkey solution. A ninja strategy. Instead, the following are proven methods of increasing your readership consisting of visitors, subscribers, and customers for years to come.

Two Ways to Get People To Your Website

There are two types of traffic to your website: earned traffic and paid traffic. There is no such thing as free traffic. Interestingly enough, most of the people I see online only use one strategy. They either focus on creating such great content that they will eventually be found through organic search (earning it), or they focus primarily on paying to run ads (paying for it). I believe that, in order for you to increase your impact and your income, you need to have a blend of traffic.

Your Perfect Traffic Blend

Your perfect traffic blend is a mixture of both earned and paid traffic. Never rely solely on one source of traffic. Most of the people I see online who only use one strategy are only using earned traffic. They have SEO on the brain, so they spend their time and energy creating epic blog posts. They create podcasts. These people generate "top of mind awareness" in order to build up the numbers of people visiting their website. But paid traffic can also be a great medium for growing your visitors in very specific niches.

Earned Traffic

Organic search is the process of someone typing in keywords or phrases related to what you talk about on your website. For example, if you are an attorney in Tampa, Florida, someone living in Tampa who goes to Google and types in "attorney" is likely to find your website. This is organic search. There is nothing you really did to specifically optimize your website to help people find it, yet they found it because your content was relevant to what they're looking for.

Search engine rankings

Just for fun, do a test. Think about the keywords that someone would type in if they were searching for your latest blog post. If you don't have a blog, then use the search engine terms for keywords that someone would use if they were trying to find your website.

Using the previous example involving Krista, a visitor might search "encouraging verses for women." If you search the terms "encouraging verses for women", would you find Krista's blog? That is the question. So take some time and type terms in your search engine to figure out if your site is showing up in the results. As far as I'm concerned, your site needs a shot in at least the top five results. Many people strive to be on the first page of Google. However, the reality is the majority of people that click are going to click on one of the first five results, likely the number one or number two result. So the best thing that you can do is get ranked as high as possible in the search engine results to increase the number of people who are going to find your content.

Earned traffic is based on organic search. When somebody searches for your product by keywords, the earned traffic strategy is to make sure that your content rises to the top. However, at the end of the day, this search engine optimized content, otherwise known as content that the search engines like and want to promote, is based on the top three characteristics:

- First, the content is on topic.
- Second, the content has social proof. In other words, other people are linking to that content and enjoying it.
- Third, the content is valuable. You can have content that's on topic and people link to, but if it doesn't have value, it can not have staying power.

Value can be divided into three categories: Inspirational, Actionable, and Empowering.

All good content either inspires, educates, informs, and/or empowers. It either gets you excited about something, teaches you exactly how to do something, or informs you as to the fact that you could do something.

So earned traffic comes as a result of someone searching on Google, someone seeing a social share like a retweet on Twitter or a Like on Facebook, somebody forwarding the content or telling you at a conference, "Hey, you gotta check out that Brian Dixon. He has some really good content!" All of that is earned: you generated traffic simply because you did your job.

Four additional tips

1. Create a website that solves a clearly defined problem for a highly targeted audience.
2. Build a Proverbs 27:2 strategy: "Let another praise you, and not your own mouth; a stranger, and not your own lips." Develop a strategy that enables that other party bragging to happen consistently.
3. Advertise consistently to a highly targeted audience to generate awareness and entice the first visit.
4. Convert visitors to subscribers on their first visit.

Referral links

This is when someone "recommends" your site by sharing a link, posting on social media, or mentioning you or your brand on their podcast. It also has the added benefit of social proof.

Paid Traffic

The second form of traffic is paid traffic. You may want to consider adding a form of paid traffic to your traffic blend. Especially if you are just starting out, paid traffic may be a great way to help get your brand off the ground. I am particularly excited about paid traffic and believe that it should always be part of your strategy, no matter how much earned traffic you already have, because paid traffic is the best way to engage a targeted audience. You decide who will see your stuff.

We know that ads are generally interrupters but, with paid traffic, you can decide who you're going to interrupt. If you do it the right way, you're actually offering them something they were already looking for.

Would you like a free sample?

A real world example of this is the Japanese noodle house at the mall. As you're walking to the food court deciding what you're going to eat, a friendly restaurant worker walks up to you and asks, "Would you like to try our sesame chicken?" She hands you a little piece of hot, fresh, delicious, sesame chicken. You're pleasantly surprised, thankful, and you pop it into your mouth. Consequently, you might end up deciding to eat at the Japanese noodle house.

When she handed you the piece of chicken, you didn't say, "How dare you interrupt me!" Instead, it was the right offer in the right place at the right time, and she actually helped you make a buying decision.

That is what paid traffic is. By putting the right message in front of people who are already interested in your type of message, you're actually serving them. For example, struggling authors need to know if they should pursue a traditional publisher or self-publish. There are many considerations, and the entire process can be pretty confusing. So a webinar teaching you the advantages of self-publishing over traditional publishing would be something valuable to first-time authors who are just starting out. If you were to see a Facebook ad inviting you to attend a free webinar to learn about the advantages of self-publishing, that would be like a little nugget of sesame chicken.

The point is this: You do not need to have a blog that never receives any new visitors. You need a strategy for recruiting these new visitors, and organic traffic and referrals from friends and family can only get you so far. In other words, if you really want to grow your blog or get your message out, you need to get in front of your ideal audience. You can cross your fingers and hope that people are going to share your awesome content or you can take matters into your own hands and advertise directly to your target audience. Bottom line: Do something. You spent enough time and effort on creating that content. It makes no sense that you would not spend time or money promoting it.

The average person has never purchased advertising before. So it makes sense that many bloggers and other content creators would be opposed to running ads on Facebook and other social media. It makes sense because the perspective is understandable. Why would I advertise something I'm giving away for free?

I have a very simple response to that question. Advertising drives new visitors. New visitors create the opportunity to gain subscribers and subscribers create the opportunity to make sales by converting them into customers. A line can be drawn from advertising to visitors to subscribers to customers.

A few tips on advertising online:

1. Don't advertise unless you have something to sell, but remember that selling something involves a free lead magnet which we'll discuss further. Advertising should follow a sequence, which can be accelerated or decelerated depending on the visitors' engagement level.
2. Advertising should have a very clear purpose. You have a product or program to sell and you have a clearly defined audience who may want to buy.
3. You position your project or program in front of your preferred audience with an enticing offer.
4. Your audience makes a decision. On Facebook, they can make the following decisions: Ignore your ad, click LIKE on your ad, click LIKE on your page, click the picture on your ad to visit your landing page, click the link in your ad text description to arrive at your landing page, click the call to action button such as "sign up," "download," or "learn more" to arrive at your landing page.

Warnings about paid traffic:

Do the math. If it costs two dollars per click, how many clicks could you get for $20? That's right: just 10. If you convert 6% of your website visitors into subscribers how many visitors will you need to get one subscriber? That's right more than 10, which means that you can waste $20 getting zero subscribers and zero customers. Feels a little bit like gambling, doesn't it? This is why people are very wary of paid traffic. Sometimes, it feels like you're spending money and just throwing it down a big, dark hole. In this section, I hope to offer advice that prevents this feeling.

No clear call to action

Another mistake people make with paid traffic is that they neglect to include a clear call to action. You need to set up an expectation of what somebody's hoping to accomplish by clicking your ad. This works really well with the

FLOATS model because you're offering a lead magnet when they opt in. Your ad is simply your FLOATS model, which allows you to say, "Is this your problem? Download the solution by clicking here".

For example, Parker can create an advertisement for any social media platform with a seven-step cold call checklist: "Do you hate cold calls? Download this seven step cold call checklist to help you." That's all you have to say. The people who want to get some help when it comes to cold calls will click. When Parker follows up with an email autoresponder nurturing campaign to tell these new subscribers a little bit more about who he is and prove that he can inject more value into their lives, he is nurturing the subscribers to become the ideal customer for his sales training course. In fact, some of them might be so poised to buy that they're going to skip the entire email campaign and check out Parker's course right away.

Not split testing

Another mistake I see people make when paying for traffic is that they are not split testing their advertisements. Creating one advertisement is fine. Creating two with one slight variation is even better. Always set up a baseline and a challenge. Once you have a clear result, then set up another challenge with one small tweak or change to the ad.

Where to advertise on Social Media

Finding the best place to acquire paid traffic for your online business is half of the battle. You have several choices when it comes to advertising on social media, but these are the most well-known.

Twitter

Twitter is a mostly mobile platform. People are scanning Twitter looking for the latest news, checking in on what their friends are talking about, and browsing for interesting resources. Creating an ad on Twitter can be a great place to promote your product or resource. Twitter allows for specific targeting, including people who follow a certain person. This way you can make sure that the only people who see your ad are already aware of your industry and have an interest in it.

Facebook

Facebook is the mother ship. When you talk about online advertising, especially on social media, Facebook is the place to be. Every few months I hear people complaining about how advertising on Facebook never works, yet people still willingly spend money advertising on Facebook. The reality of Facebook, and really any other social media platform, is that you want to be where the people are. Since almost everyone is using Facebook, you want your brands to be there as well. There are specific tips to saving money on Facebook ads and doing some better targeting. Experts in the field include Amy Porterfield and John Loomer, both of whom have amazing free resources available at their respective websites.

Best practices for paid ads

Targeted audience

A billboard is not targeted (besides geographically). A handshake is very targeted (you can only shake one, or maybe two at a time). Targeting your ads is like going for the handshake. You are seeking out the ideal person to meet and youintroducing yourself to them personally instead of just standing on a chair in the middle of a crowded room and yelling, "Buy my stuff."

Clear Call to Action

A great ad has a clear CTA, or Call to Action. It needs to be instantly clear what benefit someone will receive by clicking on your ad. This is why paid ads are so aligned to the FLOATS model. All you do is present your Lead Magnet to a targeted group of people. "Hey, if you are struggling with x, then you need y. Click here to get y." That is what your ads should read like.

Custom landing page

Never send ad traffic to a generic page (like the home page) on your website. Instead, send the people who click on your ad to a custom landing page you set up for that particular ad. This way, you know exactly why they are at that page and where they came from. You can even personalize the page to say, "Welcome to this page. Thanks for checking us out on Facebook. To download the Lead Magnet, just click here." See how easy that is?

Google Adwords

When it comes to advertising online, Google Adwords is the grandpa. It's been around quite a long time and it's not as efficient as it used to be. Google Adwords allows you to bid based on search traffic. This could be a great resource for you, especially if you have a product or program to sell. For example, if someone is looking for ideas for curriculum for eight Bible study lessons, Nicole might create a Google Adwords campaign with "Bible study curriculum" as the keywords. The more specific and niche you are on Google Adwords, the better.

YouTube

Advertising on YouTube. YouTube is a video platform, which means that ads on YouTube are video ads. I love video. In fact, I have a whole course called Video Blog Academy, which teaches you about online video. Check it out at videoblogacademy.com. Advertising on YouTube is very fun and rewarding. The reason for that is because nothing tells your story in a more powerful way than video. YouTube now enables you to become the Tony Robbins of your day by simply building your business off of infomercials. Except in Tony's day, you could not target these ads. So his 3 AM infomercials would play to anyone that had a television on. However, you can create an ad specifically focused on certain people through keywords, customer segments, and interest. Since YouTube is owned by Google, there are some cross-platform opportunities between Adwords and YouTube advertising. The basic point is this: find some great resources you can follow online and try a $20 test. You never know how well you might do.

Retargeting

My favorite type of online advertising to help generate paid traffic is called retargeting.

Retargeting is when you place an ad in front of someone who has already visited your website. The reason this is so powerful is that they indicated an interest in what you have to offer. Many programs now allow retargeting where you create a custom list of people comprised only of those who have already visited your website. This is accomplished through a pixel code that is placed on your website and is saved on the browser history of your website visitors. Once they have the pixel code on their computer, it now shows up when they're browsing the Internet. For example, your ad would appear on multiple websites, including the major ones like CNN or ESPN.com.

Basic guidelines for successful online advertising:
- Start small.
- Set a fixed budget.
- Constantly test new things.
- Don't give up.

It's easy to get frustrated by online advertising, but the reality is that it works. These are the best practices, and in order to master the skills, you need to learn these best practices. You can learn from other people's experiences but sometimes you just need to get in the game. Set a small budget and get started.

What about social media?

Using additional outposts to entice visitors to your website:

Although the majority of this book is going to focus on your Wordpress website, it is important to acknowledge the fact that people might find you from your social media platforms first. So, in the next few pages we will break down each of the major five social media platforms and speak specifically about ways that you can use these platforms to drive traffic back to your website.

That's the basic philosophy. You want a website that converts visitors to subscribers and then an email campaign that converts subscribers to customers. You can use social media as a way to entice people to visit your website.

Because of the short character limitations of Twitter there are three major ways my clients and I have optimized the service.

1. Direct outreach to decision-makers. For the most part, the actual person associated with their brand manages their own Twitter account. This is usually not true of their website or email address. Thus, Twitter is a great tool for reaching out directly to decision makers in your niche. As an example, you might use Twitter to reach out to a blogger to propose a guest post. Writing a guest post featured on their blog can help drive traffic back to your website.
2. Personal learning community. A second way we have optimized Twitter is as a personal learning community. Because of the limited character length, links are great content on Twitter. People love to share actual articles such as "Five Reasons Not To Do This" or "Ten Tools To Use For That". By sharing this content and adding #hashtags related to your niche, you can get retweets and gain followers, which can ultimately lead new people to click through your links. A favorite tool for sharing links to other people's content is snip.ly. This tool allows you to attach a message to the page, and you can even include a link back to your own site. Check it out.

3. Event-centric outreach. The third way to use Twitter is to gain followers around an event. If there is an industry event, even if you're not able to physically attend, you can follow #hashtags during the convention or conference. Just by retweeting people that are at the event or asking questions through Twitter using the main #hashtag, you can gain followers who will be more likely to click on links to your own original content in the future.

It's also important to note that conference attendees are an ideal segment of your niche audience because they have demonstrated a willingness both to spend money and take action on that content, thus implying that they have a budget and may be a great candidate for your products or programs.

YouTube

YouTube is the world's second most popular search engine. Because YouTube is owned by Google you can benefit into places by having great actual content posted in the form of a video. And video doesn't have to be complicated. Using something as basic as QuickTime player, you can make a new movie recording and simply talk through a series of slides about your niche, which you can then post on YouTube. Because the general impression is that YouTube requires a greater investment of time, equipment, and financial resources, the competition is far less on YouTube then it is for a standard website, or even an Instagram follow. And let's not forget, people simply love videos. I would much rather watch a video about my niche then read an article.

Something else to consider about YouTube

Since video is a much more personal medium (because you can see someone's face and hear their voice), you can make a deeper connection with your audience than you normally would through your own writing.

One of my favorite parts of YouTube is YouTube advertising. When someone clicks on a certain keyword or phrase on YouTube, you can have your video display before their video. Think about how powerful that it is. Using Parker as an example, he can play his video in front of a video on top sales techniques. This way, he knows that his advertisement is only being shown to people who are about to watch a video with sales techniques. Parker can create a video with a few of his tips followed by a call to action to download a free lead magnet to help the viewer.

Instagram

Instagram is my favorite social network. Instagram is a very visual social platform.

I've seen it work really effectively with a picture about your blog or you, a product, a strategic, mini-blog post description or story, and 4 to 6 very targeted #'s which are focused on your keywords.

Here are a few tips for using Instagram to drive traffic

Use the phrase "link in profile" in your description. This will get people to click on your profile and click on the link. I would recommend sending people to a mobile optimized page from your Instagram account such as "YourName.com/mobile".

Following

Another great strategy for growing traffic on Instagram is following other people in your niche. When you have a great targeted content they are much more likely to follow you back.

Apply The 8:1 Principle

Make sure that you post at least eight valuable posts on Instagram before posting something promotional. Train your audience to expect great posts from your Instagram account and they'll take notice when you post a link to a lead magnet from your Instagram account.

Use Video

Video is still fairly uncommon on Instagram. By using animated photos that have text or even narration you can increase engagement. There's something very tempting about pressing play on an Instagram post and can dramatically increase your likes which leads to more follows and eventual clicks back to your site.

Facebook

The key to succeeding on Facebook is to consider what would make a better experience for my audience? Since Facebook is constantly changing, many of my clients have been affected by unannounced changes and they've seen a big drop in traffic coming from Facebook. Every time Facebook releases a new update to their algorithm (the way that they decide which content appears on your newsfeed), they mention in their press release their "ongoing effort to improve the user experience". The best thing you can do on Facebook is to use the latest features that Facebook is promoting such as, at the time of this writing, make a video on Facebook and find ways to engage your audience using that tool. Ask people to comment, like, and share your content. Facebook monitors action. When your posts help encourage engagement from your fans, your post will show up more frequently in their newsfeed.

The number one way we use Facebook with our clients is Facebook advertising. This allows you to place your message in front of the eyes of your ideal audience even if they are not already following you on Facebook. We could spend an entire book on Facebook ads alone, but the main takeaway is this: the goal of any social media account is to get people to click back to your website to download your lead magnet and be added to your email list. Anything you can do to encourage more people to sign up for your email list will help you grow your business.

Other social networks

Pinterest, Snapchat, Periscope, and whatever's next!

New social networks are popping up fairly frequently. But the basic rules still apply. Create great content. Offer a compelling magnet for your target audience and engage authentically in your niche. If you follow those rules, you can't go wrong.

Social sharing

You know all those social media buttons that you see on blogs? Those enable your visitors to share your content on their social media profiles. The most common are Facebook, Twitter, sometimes LinkedIn, and Pinterest. Social sharing is a great way to drive more traffic to your blog. If your content is good and people find value, they are very likely to share it with their audience, even if their audience is made up of just a few hundred Facebook friends. There are many ways to make your blog social sharing friendly.

Which channels to focus on?

With so many social media channels available, it's hard to know which ones to focus on. The simple answer is that you should "be everywhere" (credit to Pat Flynn), making sure that your content shows up wherever your ideal clients hang out online. This means Facebook, Twitter, Instagram, and your own website. If your audience is on Twitter, you should start using Twitter. If your audience is on Facebook, use Facebook. However, your audience will probably be segmented into a percentage on Twitter, a percentage on Instagram, and a percentage on Facebook, so you should use each of the methods your audience uses to engage them.

Focus on a few

If you look at "namechk.com", you'll notice that there are several hundred social media platforms. I'm not suggesting that you try to make it big on all of these. Instead, use Google Analytics on your website to figure out the top three sources of traffic and work on maximizing those.

When I look at the incoming traffic reports on Google analytics for most of our clients, I notice that the majority of traffic is coming from direct links on Facebook and Twitter. This convinces me that this is how the audience is currently finding the website. It doesn't mean that it is the only way they should, so it may be worth exploring and testing other tools. However, since the audience is already using these sites, it's important that I maximize that.

A unified experience

As you look at the first impression of people coming to your site, consider the user experience. Who are they? Where are they coming from? If they're coming from Twitter, does your website still feel like a unified experience? If they're coming from Facebook, does your website fit that same unified experience?

Just like a store

Let's go down a side tangent for a minute to flesh this out a little bit more. Every city that I've lived in has had two primary shopping malls: the old one and the new one. The old one used to be the cool mall about 20 years ago, but when the new one was built, all of the major stores moved to the new mall.

The old mall is still around but has fewer and fewer stores. You notice that the old mall begins to have many vacancies, which drives down the cost of rent and attracts start-up boutiques. These are stores started by a local person who is missing some basic awareness of merchandising, branding, marketing, and advertising. Walking through the mall, you can instantly tell which stores are supported by a national brand and which stores are a local mom-and-pop store.

From the sign above the door to the way that the store is laid out to the cash register itself, the mom-and-pop stores have a lower quality about them. They just don't quite fit into the mall, and, if they do and this is the new norm for this mall, then it is clear to everyone that the mall's days are limited.

In the same way, your website, like it or not, is being compared to the big boys. People are going to look at your website from the same computer screen that they visit all of the other professional sites. You are competing with CNN, ESPN, TechCrunch, Target.com, and all of the other sites that your audience visits on a regular basis. Unless you have a very specific reason to do differently, let your design and formatting fit in. Be a great mall store prototype.

Follow the rules that are clearly laid out by three or four other benchmark websites. You do not have to be unique in your design and user experience. Be unique in the content. Let the content stand on its own.

The franchise prototype design

In his wonderful book, The E-Myth Revisited, Michael Gerber talks about the franchise prototype. When building a business poised for growth, you don't just want to build one location, but you want to build a system that can be replicated at many locations.

This way of thinking also applies to your online business. Focus on systems and replication. Treat your website like the franchise prototype of your next website. Set the standard high for what you put on your website. Treat your site like the first mall store locations. From the colors to the branding to the user interface and design, the decisions you're making right now will impact the future decisions you make about your website. So take the time to ensure that they are the highest quality possible.

Let's talk about a couple of examples:

A book launch is a really clear launch. You have a publication date. You put together a campaign, invite people on your list so that they can have something special, and eventually those people buy the book.

The second example is a course launch. What I do with a number of my clients is launch a Facebook ad and autoresponder campaign to a live webinar Q&A. After that, I'll launch a similar campaign for the sale of an online course which leads to the fulfillment of that online course. From there, we build a nurture list which receives further offers from us over time.

To start today, let me walk you through the six steps of the FLOATS model. For those who are just starting out, this is a great way for you to build your list. I would always recommend a low-price information product just to get your list started. Then, as you grow in your business building journey, this model will continue to work for you.

There are many ways to improve the way your website shows up in search engine results . This is called SEO, or search engine optimization. We won't give major focus to search engine optimization in this book, but here are a few basic principles:

Create high-quality, relevant content consistently. That's it - one sentence to explain how to increase your organic search results.

Let's take a minute to break that down.

High-quality

It used to be that you could just create content and it didn't have to be high-quality. For example, you could just stuff your website with keywords where you would use the same word multiple times and your search engine results would increase based on this tactic. That is not true anymore. There are many ways that search engines rank and rate your content. Therefore, the best way to ensure a good ranking is create great high-quality content.

Characteristics of high-quality content include:

- Clear paragraphs and introductions.
- Bullet points with key steps or principles laid out in plain English.
- A call to action inviting engagement from your audience such as a question or an invitation to share after they read the article.

References to other quality content online

Instead of just using your own head to create your content, cite other sources. This is called "backlinking", where you are sharing content from other blogs and other blogs are linking to you. Search engines love high-quality content that references other high-quality content.

Multimedia

High-quality content engages multiple modalities. Instead of just having someone read your blog, wouldn't it be awesome if they could also listen to it or watch a video about that topic? Because video takes more work than just typing words, you also have less competition for ranking.

Relevant content

Content that is relevant focuses on the reader and avoids the curse of knowledge.

No matter what you write about, you likely have the curse of knowledge, which means you forget what it's like to be a beginner and what the basic skills or terms are that people need to know. Since you work in your industry on a daily basis, it's hard to picture yourself as a beginner. However, when you write for a beginner, your content is more relevant.

Relevant content focuses on the reader and not on the writer. As the writer, you have your own perspective, but you need to think about how you can help enable or assist the reader in accomplishing his or her goals. Relevant content gets read and relevant content gets shared. Relevant content will receive higher search engine results.

Consistency

If I had to choose just one piece of advice in this area of focus, it would be the consistency factor. If you are trying to gain traffic and a following from your blog, the best thing you can do is post every day. That's right, every single day. Even if you're writing only 3 to 5 sentences per day, you will develop the habit of writing. Your readers will develop the habit of visiting your blog. You'll get better, they will know you more, and you will gain traction. High-quality content shared once a year might gain some traction and even "go viral", but what does it matter if you have nothing to lead people into?

So get consistent in what you post. That will make the biggest difference. By creating high-quality, relevant content consistently you will begin to drive more traffic.

Search engine optimized

When your website or blog is search engine optimized, it means that people searching for that kind of content can find it easily. Basically, what happens is that your site is indexed by search engines. Search engines have programs that search the web looking for new content. Once they recognize that you have new content available, it will begin to show up in search engine results. Depending on the size of your blog and how often it is indexed, it may take a couple days for your new content to show up when someone searches for it.

Improving the first impression

Remember the importance of the first impression - measure and improve the web visitors' first impression of the program based on their experience at the website.

- When a visitor lands on your website, where are they directed to go?
- What is their first impression of the program based on the materials presented?
- In what ways can the user experience be improved?

Everything on your website can be tracked and measured. Here is how and why you should measure your website:

Three Quick Ways to Improve your Website

1. Move to a self-hosted WordPress website.
This allows for custom editing, installing plug-ins, and ownership of your files.

2. Add a lead magnets giveaway with an opt-in to your email newsletter.
Following the FLOATS model (which you can download on our website at dixonagency.org), you want a lead magnet that is attractive, enabling, and focuses on what your customer wants.

3. Benchmark your website.
Choose three colleagues in your field and use their websites as a benchmark for your website. At least once a month, review any changes they've made to their website including design, functionality, and content, and consider how you might adjust your site to better engage your audience.

Benchmark your website

One sure way to continually improve your website and make sure that you have a golden first impression is to benchmark your website. Benchmarking your website involves choosing three competitors' sites to compare yourself against. Instead of starting from scratch and trying to build your own site 100% from scratch, use the counsel of others. For example, mix up your color scheme. Instead of just picking your favorite colors to use on your website, look at the colors every other competitive website uses. What you might find are common characteristics.

For example, when it comes to purchasing, the checkout button is usually yellow or orange. This is helpful to know. If the other three websites all use a yellow checkout button and you use a blue one, what do you think the visitor experience will be? Do you think that they'll be confused or that you'll stand out in a positive way? By making decisions based on the counsel of others, you can be more confident that you're not making some glaring errors or mistakes and missing opportunities.

Choosing three benchmark sites

I recommend that you choose three sites to compare your site against. What I mean by this is that you find three other people or businesses in a similar niche that are further down the road than you are. If you're just starting out, they should have been doing it for a few years. If you're already fairly successful, look for people at the top of their game. Of course, I'm not recommending plagiarizing or copying at all. What I am recommending is that you have something to compare your website to instead of your own ideas.

When we were just starting our agency, we took on a few non-ideal clients. I guess this is just part of the cost of learning to do business. The ones who didn't turn out to be a good long-term fit were the ones who couldn't take advice. The number one piece of advice that these clients would not take is to compare themselves to other people in their industry. If you think you are so unique but you can't compare yourself to anyone in the industry, then you are delusional because the reality is your customers are comparing you to your competitors. If you're an author, readers are going to compare you to other authors. They're going to open your book and compare your book to other books they have read. No one makes decisions in a vacuum.

Not only is it frustrating to work with a client who won't take advice, I can say with 100% confidence that the clients who refuse to compare themselves to others in the industry are not going to be around very long. It's as silly as a golfer wanting to use a broomstick instead of a set of golf clubs.

Instead, there are rules to the game. Unfortunately, as in many industries, no one has written a rulebook, at least not a definitive one. The rules are always changing. So the best way to figure out the rules, to figure out what is working, is the backwards plan, or reverse engineering.

Reverse engineering success

I started with three websites that are successful. Of course, there is time, reputation, and luck to factor in, but, for the most part, if you follow the general principles of other websites in your industry that are working, yours will work over time. You may not have immediate results, but, over time, you should see an increase in impact and income.

The Anatomy of a Website

Although this is not a book about web design, we'll cover a few basic topics to establish a common understanding.

The first thing you should do is pick a few websites that you respect. As I talk about each of the different sections you should be able to identify those sections on these websites.

Above the fold

The above the fold section is everything you see on your computer screen before you have to scroll down. The term comes from the days of the printed newspaper, which was folded in half. All the headlines for above the fold are on the top half of the newspaper that you would see if the newspaper was sitting on a news stand. This is the most important information. Everything below the fold requires you to actually pick up the newspaper, unfold it, and read.

In the same way, you want to make sure that the most important information on your website is listed above the fold, or above the line where people have to scroll. The fold can also be referred to as off-screen.

If you just took a snapshot of your website when it loads up without doing any scrolling or moving down the screen, that is everything above the fold. Looking at the benchmark sites that you'll be comparing your site to, take a look at what information they have above the fold. Usually, this includes:

- The name of the site
- The name of the author
- A picture of the author
- A lead magnet and opt in opportunity
- Some sort of free giveaway
- A nice design logo or header
- A menu bar
- The title and first paragraph or two of the most recent blog post
- A detailed explanation of the site
- An enticement to scroll

How a Website Works

There are essentially three elements to a website. There are the raw files including text, images, video, and audio; there is the host server, or the computer where these files are stored, and the instructions as to how these files will appear on your website; and there is the domain name, which tells your computer where to go when you type in the website address.

Breaking it down another way, if you type dixonagency.org into the address bar on your computer, your browser will check the domain name settings, which will give a number of the IP, the Internet protocol address of the folder on a computer called a server where all of your website files are stored. Your computer will open the folder on my website server and look for an instruction file. That instruction file tells your computer exactly what to show on the screen and what happens when you click on different sections of the website.

For the sake of clarity, in this book we will be using Bluehost as the web server, Godaddy as the domain name registrants, and WordPress as the website platform. I use these three for a few reasons, mainly because they are the most popular and they are what we use with our clients each day.

Before going into the technical details, just know that we do offer support on these topics and are happy to help explain it to you or build it for you at Dixon agency.org. Remember, don't let technology get in the way of you sharing your message and serving your audience. There are others out there that have the technical expertise to help you accomplish your goals. You are a content creator. Focus on writing your content and learn just enough to get your website up and running. There's nothing wrong with hiring someone who has the expertise to take your website to the next level.

The Basic Process

You have an idea for your website, so first, choose your domain name. Your domain name is blahblahblah.com. Usually, I recommend that you own yourname.com. For those with a company or a certain brand name, you should buy that one as well. To purchase a domain, go to GoDaddy.com and type the domain name you want in the search box. If it's available, you pay $10 or so to register that domain for the first year.

Generally, I do not recommend registering a domain for more than one year because you never know how your ideas or your business will change a year from now.

What to do if your website name is taken?

If your website name is already taken, as in someone has already purchased it, you have two options:

You can either choose a different domain or you can reach out and negotiate to purchase the one you want from the person who owns it.

For example, at the time of this writing, I don't own BrianDixon.com. Brian Dixon is a fairly common name and someone bought the domain name a long time ago. When I first created my blog, I could only purchase brianjdixon.com. It's what I've been using for over 10 years and I've never had any problem with it. I'm sure there are people who try to find me by going to BrianDixon.com, but a simple Google search will reveal my real domain name. In fact, anyone looking me up is going to somehow be connected to me anyway.

Just for fun, and as an example, I reached out to the owner of briandixon.com, who by the way, doesn't really use it for anything, and told them I would buy the domain for a few hundred dollars. This is a reasonable price for this domain name. They wrote me back and said that they would sell it for $3000 and then $2000, The last time I checked they are offering it for $1200. If it really mattered to me, and it was really important that I own briandixon.com, then this would be a reasonable price.

If you're reading this and saying, "Wait a second, Brian! $1200 just for a domain name? Is that reasonable?"

The answer is that it depends. It depends on how much it's worth to you. One of my good friends was using "hisname.tv" for quite a long time. His name is fairly common, and he has been building a brand based solely on his name. He's been in negotiations with the person who has owned the ".com" version of his domain for over a year. Finally, he decided to make an out of the park offer. He scraped together all of the money he could and made a bold move, a four figure offer out of the blue.

You know what? The price was accepted! Think about it from the other end. Someone bought the domain name, hoping to either use it themselves or sell it later. The idea of selling it later is really going away. It's nice to have a .com; however, for the most part; you can get away with a .tv, a .net, or just using some configuration of your name that's a little different. People will still find you.

My recommendation is not to let the domain name stop you from conducting business online. You can always save up and buy a domain name later. So, if the .com is not available, don't worry. Just by a variation of yourname.com, yourname.net, yourname.us, yourname.tv. You can always upgrade later.

Website Hosting

Now that you have your own domain name, you need a place to host your files. This is called the server, essentially a computer somewhere, likely in San Francisco, where you upload your files. Those files are then copied into a network of hosting servers so that the distance between the file and the computer of your website visitor is as short as possible.

When choosing a hosting company, you want to find someone who is both cheap and reliable. My favorite hosting company to use is called BlueHost. They have a network of servers all over the world, their delivery system is very reliable, and their help desk is awesome.

To get started, simply go to bluehost.com and sign up for a hosting account. To make things simple, you could even buy your domain name through BlueHost so everything is integrated. On average, you're going to spend $10 per year for your domain and $10 per month for your hosting. With BlueHost, this even includes your email address, which you can get at yourname.com. So the overall investment to get your website up and running, skills aside, is about $150 a year. If you look at that number and think, "That capital is too big for me to create a website," you should probably be reading another book.

Website Platform

Now that you have your domain name to point to a server and a server to host your files, you need a website platform, which will serve as the instructions for your website. To really simplify it, compare it to building a house. The host is the land you build on, the files are the raw materials that go into your website like brick and wood go into a house, and your platform is the house blueprint.

LEAD MAGNET

A lead magnet is content you give away to your website visitors in exchange for their email address. The content needs to be valuable enough for someone to give you their email address and be added to your email list in exchange for that content. Lead magnets are the key to growing your business online.

In this chapter you will learn:

- 10 different types of lead magnets
- 5 characteristics of effective lead magnets
- Technology to delivery the lead magnet
- Tips for presenting the lead magnet on your page

Why you need a lead magnet?

The majority of people who visit your website will never return. Even producing consistent content is not enough to get visitors to come back to your blog. People are busy. There is always something else that is new and shiny to look at online. The best action your visitors can take on your website is to opt-in to your email list. This way, you can continue the conversation with them, even if they never return to your website.

So what is a lead?

A lead is another way to say prospect, subscriber, or potential customer. Leads are people who could turn into potential sales. This could be the sale of your book, a ticket to your conference, or even a client for your consulting services. Whatever it is you have to offer, you want to convert casual visitors into subscribers and nurture those subscribers into customers.

Lead magnet tips

- Any lead magnet is better than no lead magnet. Many authors and bloggers online offer no incentive for people to sign up for their email newsletter. Instead, they simply say, "Stay in the loop - subscribe to updates." There's no value in this. Unless your content is so good that they are dying to read your updates, you need to give them a little something extra.
- Establish a clear call to action (CTA) to invite visitors to subscribe. You might create a sidebar graphic that simple states "click here to download my free x."
- Consider the needs of your ideal customer avatar client and create a lead magnet that encourages them to opt-in. Depending on the needs of the ideal prospect, a lead magnet may include a checklist, a quiz, a downloadable article, or free training.

The Power of an email address

An email address is the most valuable piece of customer contact data you can receive. An email address allows you to directly communicate with your customer. There is no way to ignore an email. Like our mailbox at home, this is something that we check at least once a day. It is the one tool everyone uses, from celebrities to CEOs and from factory workers to stay-at-home moms. Everyone has an email address. In order to truly engage your visitors and convert them into subscribers, you need their email address. A lead magnet is the most effective way to entice visitors to send you their email address.

But I have nothing to sell

So what if you have nothing to sell right now? It is still important to capture visitors' contact information and add them to your list. One day you will have something to sell. In fact, one of the biggest mistakes first-time authors make is waiting to grow their email list. Publishers love to see that you have a growing platform - a group of people who follow you and will potentially purchase your book. Don't wait to grow your email list. Start now.

Types of Lead Magnets

There are many different types of lead magnets that you can use to entice someone to give you their name and email address. In this section, we will break down 10 lead magnets you can use. These include toolboxes, special previews, surveys and quizzes, checklists, three video preview series, downloadable PDFs, and free mini-courses.

Toolbox

A popular lead magnet to give away is a list of resources you frequently use - otherwise known as your "toolbox." No matter what your industry or topic is, there are tools that your audience will need to accomplish their goals. You can give away a list of your favorite tools to help your audience skip the learning curve and start using the right tools from day one.

There are several advantages to giving away your toolbox as a lead magnet.

1. **Easy to put together.** A toolbox is a very easy lead magnet to create. All you need to do is look at the tools you use on a regular basis and write out the list. Tools may include software applications you use, favorite websites, tangible products such as a specific kind of computer or instrument, training products you recommend such as online membership sites, live conferences, and/or books that you love.

2. **Affiliate commissions.** Another advantage of giving away your toolbox is that it can generate revenue. If you are recommending something for your audience to purchase, you can take advantage of affiliate links. An affiliate link is a commonly used practice online where you receive a small commission for recommending a product to someone to buy. For example if I recommend that you purchase a book on Amazon, I can include a live link to the Amazon store with a tracking code, which tells Amazon that the customer came from my link. Amazon then rewards me for helping them make the sale by giving me a small percentage commission of that sale. Affiliate commissions range widely depending on the vendor and the products. Amazon affiliate commissions are as low as 4%. If you recommend a $10 book, you're only making $.40 from that book. They can also be quite lucrative. Some of the online tools I recommend, like Ontraport and Infusionsoft, pay a monthly commission of $40+ per month.
3. **Expert positioning.** By giving away your list of tools, you are positioning yourself as a go-to resource for all of these tools. When one of your subscribers has questions about ANY of these tools, they are likely to reach out to you first. This is a great opportunity for you to develop blog posts and training programs around your best practices in using these tools.

A Special Preview

A second type of lead magnet you could give away is a preview of your content. For example, you might give away two or three chapters of a 12-chapter book or you might give away the first few slides from a keynote presentation with 10 slides. You could even give away the first exercise in a series of 10 exercises.

When giving away a free preview, it is important to make sure that you enable the subscriber to get access to the full content as soon as possible. A free preview usually indicates that your sale will be for the entire content. For example, if you have a book to sell, giving away the first two chapters is a great lead magnet. This allows someone try out your content and, if they like it, you can place a link at the end of the PDF to purchase the rest of the content.

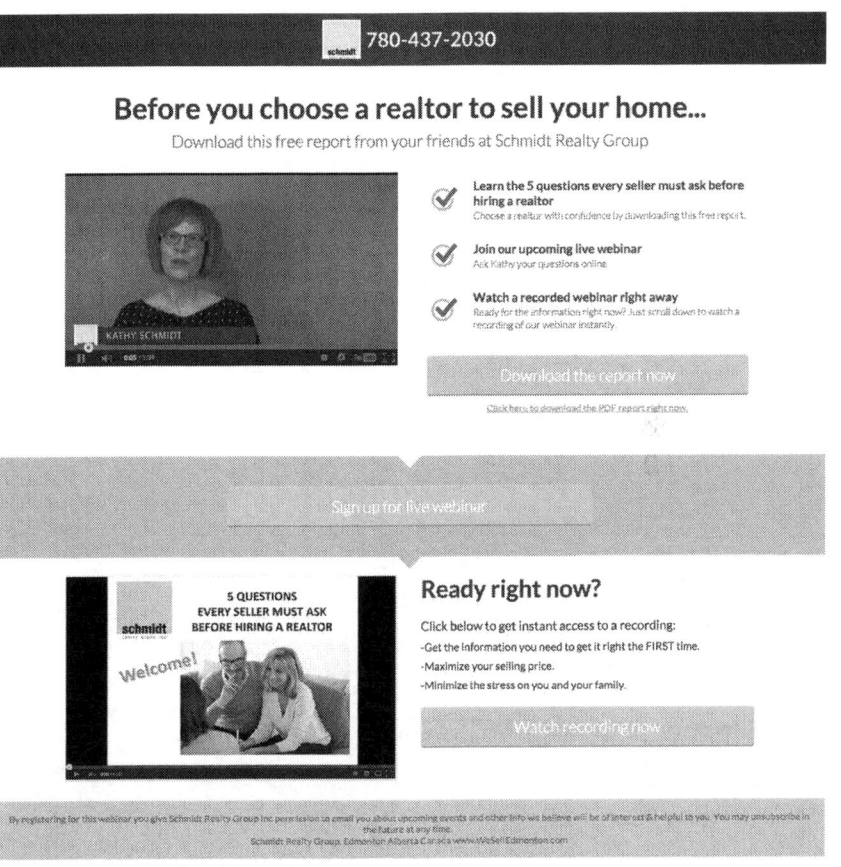

Figure 1: This lead magnet offered a free training webinar for the Realtor niche from KathySchmidt (WeSellEdmonton.com). We built this page with Lead pages and integrated with GoToWebinar and Ontraport.

Surveys and Quizzes

Another lead magnet you might offer is a fillable form such as a survey or quiz. People like to receive personalized advice, and you can use their responses to a form to better understand your customers and provide better marketing materials to them.

Surveys and quizzes help you learn more about your ideal clients. This will help you figure out what they need to accomplish their goals. You can also use leading questions to guide respondents to the next natural step. For example, "Take our Five Minute Quiz to discover your sales personality" is a great lead magnet.

Tips for Surveys and Quizzes

1. You can use a free online tool such as SurveyMonkey or Wufoo to host the form.
2. Do not require the email address at the beginning, but use it at the end for people to receive the results. They're already invested in filling out the form and will be more likely to enter their email address to find out the results at that point.

A Checklist

A checklist is perhaps the quickest lead magnet that you can possibly create. All you need to do this type out 6 to 12 bullets in a Word document and export as a PDF, and now you have a checklist! You can create your checklist in less than five minutes because you know your topic better than most and you know exactly what should be included. For example, as someone who helps authors and speakers grow their online impact and income, I might put together a checklist for a website that helps you make more sales. It might look something like this:

"Does your website sell for you? This seven step checklist will help you find out."

In the example above, you can clearly see who my target audience is and what their goals are. This enables me to effectively communicate the value of the lead magnet. I know that this lead magnet is attracting people with a website that have something to sell.

Here are a few ideas for someone who offers personal coaching:

- Seven Characteristics Of A Great Personal Coach
- Seven Ways To Know You Are Ready To Hire A Personal Coach

- Seven Ways To Not Get Screwed When Hiring A Personal Coach
- Seven Websites To Find A Personal Coach
- Seven Benefits Of Hiring A Personal Coach

Figure 2: We created this Lead Magnet for Dan Miller, offering his audience a free PDF with 18 questions to help them experience freedom in their career. This lead to an upsell page and a five email nurturing sequence.

Take a few minutes to brainstorm checklists you could create for your niche industry. Here are a few starters:

- __ tips to help you _____
- __ things _____ need to know about _____
- __ tools you need to _____

A Three-Video Series

A more advanced lead magnet is a video series. We've created these for our clients and, although they require an investment, we've have seen very good results with a free video series. Here is an outline of the content to include in a video series:

- Video 1: Introduce yourself and the problem that you solve
- Video 2: Paint a picture of life after solving the problem
- Video 3: "Imagine if" — "Well, now you can!"

Video 1 - the Problem

The first video is a biographical video showing who you are and what you've struggled through to get to where you are now. This video is a combination of a video biography and your philosophy of the world. Including your philosophy of the world will help further clarify who you work with and what you have to offer them. You shouldn't hold back in this first video, but it should truly be you. Do not overdo it. It will resonate with the people you're meant to serve. The more they get to know you, the more they'll decide whether or not you are the kind of person they want to work with.

Video 2 - the Process

If Video 1 is the "negative," as in "Here is the problem that I set out on a mission to solve," then Video 2 is about the process you take your clients through. Video 2 is all about actually teaching content. When someone watches your second video, you want them to believe that they can accomplish similar results by following a proven system. "He is likable" - You want to continue building trust and credibility by showing that you are somebody worth listening to.

Video 3 - the Plan

In the third video, introduce your solution to the problem. The solutions should be your product or service.

Let's walk through a few examples.

Parker

Parker's first video can show him in the car waiting to go into a sales appointment. The script can read something like the following:

"You know that feeling… Pit in your stomach, lump in your throat, trying to muster up the courage to walk through those doors. You've done it hundreds of times before. There's no reason this time should be any different, but, once again, the doubt creeps in.

> 'Do they even need my products?
> Are they going to cast me back out into the parking lot?
> Why am I even doing this?'

Hi, I'm Parker, and I know what it's like to be a 100% commission-based sales representative. You can call it whatever you want: "business development," "client relations," "field technician," but, at the end of the day, it's all the same: your job is to convince someone to buy something. That is one of the hardest jobs in the world, but it doesn't have to be. I used to hate sales, and, to be honest, I still hate some kinds of sales. But I'm not in sales. I'm in the people business. My job is to build relationships, and, if I build enough high-quality relationships, the referrals will come. People will figure out who I am and what I have to offer.

Of course, I'm not saying you leave it all up to chance or build your company based solely on referrals. There is a system to follow, a system I'm going to share with you in this video series, but, in today's video, we're going to focus on the mistakes to avoid. Because let's face it, we're all making them. In fact, I believe that every commission-based sales representative can triple their sales by avoiding these five common mistakes:

> Mistake number one
> Mistake number two
> Mistake number three
> Mistake number four
> Mistake number five

I hope that listening to these mistakes has been inspiring and has challenged you to consider how you might improve your sales process. That's exactly what we're going to talk about in tomorrow's video: a systematic approach. I look forward to seeing you tomorrow in the next video.

Oh, and one more thing. I have a question for you: Do you know another commission-based sales representative who could benefit from this video series? Click the share button below to make sure you share it with a friend."

That's it!

> Video 1 introduces the Problem
> Video 2 introduces the Process
> Video 3 introduces the Plan

You should be able to answer the following questions:
> If your customers had the right plan, what could be accomplished?
> If they had the right plan, who could they become?
> If they had the right plan, what results could they get?

Free mini course training

A great lead magnet is the mini course. A mini course is five short videos that help your audience understand more about what you have to offer.

Generally, the first video is the introductory video where you talk about what someone will learn in the mini course and what they will learn in each of the modules.

Module 1 can give them an overview of the content. For example, for Video Blog Academy, I created a mini course to follow this format: the first video welcomes people to the mini-course website and gives a quick introduction to who I am, adds some credibility statements, and tells them what to expect in the course. Notice that there is no selling in this course whatsoever. I tested the pages to see whether or not requiring an opt-in was worth the trouble. I then split test the pages to see if whether requiring an opt in to view the content drove down the rates of viewing.

Video 2 provides three quick tips or three short cuts. In this second module, I am proving the

value of what I offer by teaching the viewers three quick shortcuts to help them learn even more and really see the value of what I have to offer in VideoBlog Academy. The second module shares three quick editing tips I learned to show them how to save time doing video editing.

Video 3 is another training piece that helps the viewers understand even more how I can provide value to their life.

The entire purpose of the mini-course is to prove to visitors that there are things that they don't know. Things that I can teach them to get started right now.

The point of the fifth video, which I call a bonus, is to offer one more piece of training and then to go into a hard upsell. This is where you demonstrate the features and benefits of your upsell, which is usually a course.

What makes a great mini-course? Focus on the value. It enables your potential customers to take action on their goals, building out the entire system.

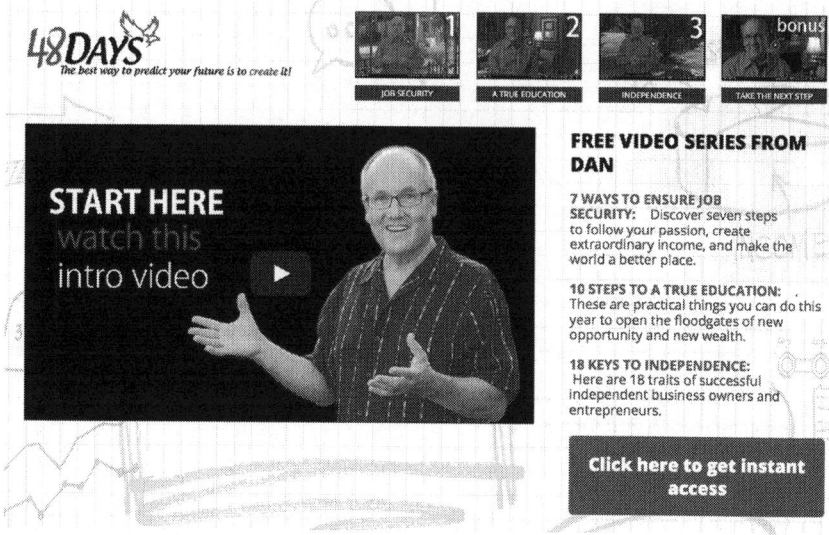

Figure 3: We created this mini-course for Dan Miller (48days.com). This serves as our main lead magnet on his site and in his email footer.

How to Build a Mini-Course

This section of the book teaches exactly how to build a mini course, but you should document the whole process. A great online sales formula is one that includes high-value training. There is nothing that builds trust and credibility like owning your platform. A great way to own your platform is to giveaway great free content that people can take action on.

My favorite way to do this is through a mini-course. Fortunately, there are technology tools available today that make creating a mini-course fairly straightforward. For this example, I'm going to use LeadPages and Ontraport, but you'll see how you could create a similar kind of course with just a simple Wordpress site and the free MailChimp application.

Essentially, here is the process:

1. Create your script.
2. Think about your models.
3. Shoot your video and edit your video into five different videos.
4. Write the content.

5. Finish building the site.
6. Think about user permissions.
7. Look at ways to drive traffic.

The great thing about building a mini course is that it can serve as an "evergreen" lead magnet. It's a great way to invite people into your free content with no risks for them. However, you can also try conversion rates based on the Facebook ads that drive traffic through your lead page.

A Lead Magnet:

- give your visitors a bite-sized piece of your training program.
- help them take the first step towards life change.

So, let's talk about your lead magnet. A lead magnet is something that attracts visitors to become a lead. The way that they become a lead is they opt in and they give you their name and email. Essentially, what they're doing is they're raising their hand. They're saying. "I want what you have to offer."

Think about what would entice your website visitors to opt-in to your email list by considering what it is they hope to accomplish. Ideally, you're helping them reach goals through a specific paid offering, but part of their journey should involve receiving something free from you. Therefore, the best lead magnet will help visitors progress in their journey towards goal actualization. By helping them move forward in their journey, they're going to receive results, and they will attribute the value of those results directly to you and your offerings. The simple psychology goes something like this: "Wow, this thing I got for free was so valuable that his paid content must be even better! I really trust when he offers me something for sale. I'm going to really think about it and probably buy it."

Another characteristic of a really good lead magnet is that it is enabling. It helps people achieve their goal. Here are a couple of examples:

A lead magnet that is a checklist: Here are the tools that I use.

A lead magnet that is a webinar: I want to teach you my seven strategies for this.

A lead magnet could be a giveaway of the audio version of the e-book that you just bought.

You get points with a lead magnet.

You need to balance the wants with the needs. If you're an expert in your space, you know what your ideal customers really need, but that might not be what they want. Think about what they want and make that your lead magnet. If they want to lose 5 pounds in five days, make that your lead magnet. If you want to teach a healthy lifestyle, including how to work out more, how to make green smoothies, or how much vitamin D they need to take, they might not want that, but that's what they need. So include that in your program, but don't make that your main selling point. You definitely cannot use it as a lead magnet. Instead, you offer something that's attractive to them, something that's enabling, something that they want. The important thing to know about a lead magnet is that you give away the "what" and then charge for the "how." For example, what they need to know about this is what you give away for free, but how to do it is what you charge for.

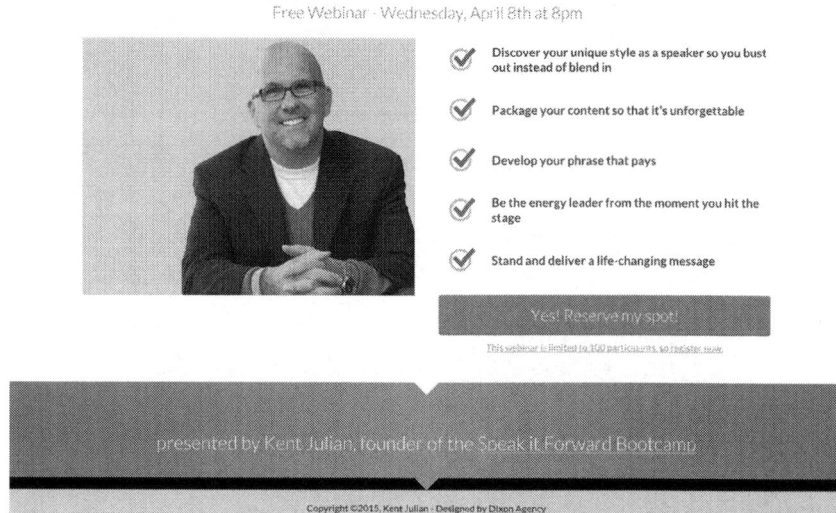

Figure 4: Facebook ads were a key strategy to drive traffic to this webinar landing page we designed for Kent Julian. This webinar lead to his premiere program SpeakItForward.me

Downloadable PDF

Most lead magnets that I see online come in a PDF, or portable digital format. A PDF is a universal file type that doesn't require special software for the user to open. They can open PDFs on their phone, on a Mac or PC, or any tablet device.

What Makes a Lead Magnet Magnetic?

A good lead magnet encourages the visitor to become a subscriber. A good rule of thumb is that the lead magnet has to be worth at least $3.00. The reason for this is simple. When someone gives you their name and email address, they are trusting you with that information and the trust costs something. If you decide to abuse that trust and post their email online or send them spam, it is inconvenient for them to try to stop that unwanted material from entering their inbox. They will need to unsubscribe. They will need to click the spam button. So a lead magnet needs to be able to overcome all of the past experiences that someone has had with spammers. This is a pretty high bar to set.

It is for this reason that I recommend your lead magnet becomes a no-brainer: "Enter your name and email here to download my FREE really cool thing!" Your offering has to be so valuable that people don't even hesitate to enter their name and email to receive it. In fact, it is worth you giving away your best content in exchange for a new email address. The reason for this is simple: Receiving an email address from a new visitor is an opportunity. It is a chance for you to communicate with them for literally years to come. If the overall lifetime customer value could be in the thousands of dollars, then giving away something really great like your book or a training program is worth their investment (their email address).

Attractive

The lead magnet has to be something that your audience wants. It should be attractive enough to encourage your visitors to subscribe. My favorite tool for creating the picture you use for your lead magnet is called Box Shot. This app allows you to take a flat image of a book cover or a checklist and create a 3D like image complete with shadows and rounded corners. This makes your lead magnet look like an actual physical product even though it's probably just a PDF document. (Tip: if you don't want to splurge for (or learn) how to use BoxShot, you can hire someone on Fiverr.com to create the 3D image for you for only five bucks. You're welcome).

Enabling

Another characteristic of a good lead magnet is that it enables your visitor to accomplish something. It will allow them to take one step closer towards their goal. Lead magnets that are enabling begin with the end in mind. What is your audience trying to accomplish? Then, working backwards, what is the first step they need to take? Your lead magnet should help them take that first step. Lead magnets that meet this criteria include a road map that shows them the 12 steps to accomplishing your goal. The first chapter of a book. The first exercise from a more in-depth program.

Want vs. Need

As experts in our respective fields, we know exactly what our audience really needs. We know how to cut the fluff and focus on the best content that's out there. Unfortunately, our audience isn't always looking for what they need, at least, not at first. They're likely focusing on what they want. The instant gratification. The quick results. Although it may feel a little counterintuitive, it's recommended that you offer them what they want at first and then include what they need in the rest of your program.

What vs. How

Give away the "what" and charge for the "how" (Credit to Stu McLaren for that concept). The "what" is a list of the items or tools someone needs to accomplish their goal. Knowing the "what" is only the first step (a piece of the machine). The real value comes in the "hows." How do you use these tools to accomplish your goal? The "what" is easy to give away and the "how" requires more in-depth training. However, once you give someone the "what", they will want to know the "hows," which makes this a great lead magnet.

For example: Parker's direct sales program might include a lead magnet that tells the sales representative what to do. For example: Make 20 contacts per day, always leave a voicemail message, and use a follow-up strategy after a face-to-face appointment. Then, in Parker's "Mastering Direct Sales for Sale" program, he goes into detail about each of these steps and teaches the "hows". How do you make 20 calls per day? How do you leave a compelling voice mail message? How do you follow up effectively? By giving away the what, Parker has piqued the interest of his audience who wants to learn more about the "hows".

OPT-IN PAGE

The opt-in page is where the visitor enters his/her name and email address in exchange for your lead magnet. In this chapter, we'll be discussing the opt-in process, which, at its most basic, involves your business prospects giving their information to you. They request your lead magnet, trusting that you won't spam them but will add value to their lives. Offering a lead magnet is only the first step in getting someone to join your list. The next step is where visitors can get stuck. You need to provide an obvious opt-in process to move your visitors forward. This is the process of opting in. It's the difference between hearing about a product that sounds interesting and actually making the purchase. If the lead magnet is the product, then the opt-in page is the store. This is where people actually making the purchase, where they actually "buy." Until they enter their name and email to download whatever you happen to be offering them, they are not yet your customers.

Make the offer clear

You need to make it clear what people are getting and what they need to do to get it. Choosing a proper lead magnet will entice people to take action and opt in, but just designing a lead magnet is not enough. Instead, you need to have a graphic which explains exactly what people need to do:

1. Click here to download the lead magnet.
2. Enter your name and email to download the lead magnet.
3. Confirm your email to download the lead magnet.

Opt in options

There are four main options you have for opt-in. The quickest and simplest one to start with is a plug-in. There are two main avenues here. The first is a hello bar, which is considered the top of your page, or you can get one at hellobar.com. Make a mental note to self to check that link.

A second option is a pop-up window or a pop up box which you can get at Pop Up Domination, LeadPages, Pop Up Alley, and many other places.

A third option for opting in is using an embedded form in the top right section of your website, where you actually take the code from the form and paste it into your website. This is what most email marketing programs such as MaleChimp and Ontraport use, and you can use one of the widgets and Wordpress to paste the HTML JavaScript code to place the form in that right top sidebar.

A fourth place to put your opt in box is at the bottom, or the footer, of your website. When people scroll to the bottom of your site, they want to take action. They're looking for something and they haven't found it yet. A fifth option for your opt-in is within your blog posts, either somewhere embedded in the text itself, which can be really effective, or at the bottom of your blog post.

As you can see, the general point is this: you want to give as many opportunities as possible without annoying people to allow your website visitors to become subscribers. After all, this is the reason you have a website in the first place. You have an audience to serve and a message to share, and the most effective way to share that message is through email. So the best thing that you can do is get people's email addresses. The best way to get their email addresses is to ask for them and the best way to ask for them is to give them something worth exchanging their email address for. This is your lead magnet.

The opt in box or a bar or page is simply completing the transaction of presenting the lead magnet, receiving the email address, and making the exchange.

Opting In

Opting in is is a big deal, and it's worthy of this entire chapter. So now we're going to get practical and share the proven methods of acquiring subscribers. This is the process where you move a visitor to a subscriber. We're going to take this time to make sure that you understand the psychology behind opting in as well as the exact tools you'll need for your own opt-in.

The rules of opting in

The reality is that the trust factor is very weak when you offer something to someone in exchange for their email address. People are burnt out. They are tired of being spammed. They feel cheated by continually giving their email address to people who have taken advantage of it and they no longer trust the transaction. You're not competing against yourself. You're competing against all of the false promises made by spammers throughout the years.

People are tired of it. They no longer want to have to deal with unsubscribing to unsolicited emails. So it is important that you are able to convince your visitors that you will take care of them and that they can trust you to give them just the right amount of information in an ethical way.

This is a lot to ask. To accomplish all of this in an email opt-in box or on a pop up can be quite difficult. So don't be discouraged to know that you're fighting a losing battle and, as people continue to get savvier online, it'll be even harder to make the trade of your lead magnet for someone's opt-in.

I know this for sure: a clear and valuable lead magnet results in the exchange of an email address for a download. This type of transaction still works and can help you dramatically grow your business.

The tools you need for opting in

The first thing you'll need for an opt-in feature on your website is an email opt-in program. At the end of this entire sequence, the purpose is to get someone on your email list so you'll want a program that manages such a list. If you don't have such a program, I recommend you start with MailChimp. It is free and simple to set up and you can really grow your list with this tool. They have a premium model where it's free to get started and then you can pay to add additional features.

From MailChimp you will need the following:

- Creating a list
- Creating an opt in page
- Creating the sequence

With MailChimp, you can copy the given code (which is often displayed on their version of a sign-up form), and decide how you want to customize this form. Don't be deterred by the directions. It doesn't have to be a complicated ordeal. You simply create the form, copy the code, paste the code on to your website, and that's it. The entire process runs itself.

There are many other programs that allow for these functions: opt-in form, delivery of the lead magnet, and adding a subscriber to a nurturing campaign. Having worked with dozens of clients and hundreds of consulting clients, I would recommend MailChimp to start and then, when you're ready for more advanced sequencing, including customer relationship management, you need to tag your subscribers and put them on a customized list before moving to Ontraport or InfusionSoft. You can learn more about these advanced tools on our website, dixonagency.org/tools.

- the page where the visitor actually enters their name and email
- help your audience reach their goals through your lead magnet

So to recap: when someone decides to click to download your lead magnet, they need to opt in. Opting in is the process of entering your name and email in exchange for the free thing.

Here are some best practices for opting in:

Require the minimum amount of information. A standard offer requires a first name and an email address. This is good enough for you to personalize follow-up emails and to make sure they get delivered to the right address. There are a few implications to this:

1. You have an opportunity to personalize emails. We'll talk more about this in the auto responder section, but, whenever you send an email, always include a foreign field for somebody's first name. It's better when you get an email and it really feels like it's coming directly from one person to you. This is possible when you use the fields creatively. In fact, the more personalized email interaction, the greater your open rates and the better your response rates.

You want to try to get as much information as possible without a decline in opt-in percentage.

Opt-in percentage is the percentage of people that decide to give their information and actually enter their information once they land on your opt in page. Various factors affect an opt-in rate. There may be an issue with the technology - perhaps it isn't mobile friendly - or there isn't a streamlined process for your visitors. You could be asking for too much information. I've also seen people require an email address in the first name field or utilize an opt-in page that doesn't match the leading to page.

The key to ensuring a high percentage of opt-ins is to create a baseline that proves the app's suggestions and then create several split tests for thorough results.

Add two definitions in the back split testing. This is where you have more than one version of the page and you track performance, letting the winner become the default page.

Requiring the minimum asking for the maximum

On several occasions, a content writer has had an offer that I want to engage in. However, these offers often fall short of my expectations. In other words, I would like to give them more information than they are asking for. This is especially true when I am a new member of the community.

An example of this is when I went to a three-day conference for the first time. The conference featured an author who I reall respected. I had read two of his books, heard him on multiple podcast interviews, watched him a few times on YouTube, but never had the opportunity to meet him personally. When I registered for the conference, it seemed that there would be a small group interaction and breakout groups, and I wanted to make sure that I was put in the right group.

The form asked for some very basic information. I would have told him pretty much anything he wanted to know, especially because I was willing to provide him with future business. The conference was only a few hundred dollars, but I liked the stuff so much that I was willing to invest even more to get results. Actually, I was interested in more than a conference ticket - I was interested in a secondary offer. He could have used the form to make one. Whether it was group coaching, an additional conference day, a follow up membership site, additional workbooks or products, or even a coach certification program, I was already sold. I would have paid another $50 to have a phone conversation with him and ask a question or two. Think about that. One phone call would have taken an extra hour of his time, but it would have been an opportunity to upsell all the people that bought the extra conference call. If just 20 attendees showed an interest in purchasing a call, he would have made at least an additional $1000.

The same is true of you. There are people in your niche that want to engage in a deeper way and you are not letting them. The only way to know this besides blindly guessing in the dark is to ask. One of the best ways to ask is on the original opt-in page. As an example, for one of my clients who has been in the online space for quite a long time, I added a "Say Hello" page. The "Say Hello" page is an opportunity for someone to write back in to introduce themselves. How often do we only think about ourselves on websites and not about our audience?

This is an opportunity for people who are already engaged and are already reading this client's About Me page to introduce themselves. It is only natural that, after reading somebody's About Me page, you want to talk about yourself. You might notice connections and want to reach out to that particular expert, even just to say hi.

With the right system, which we'll talk about more in this book, something like on support or a customer relationship management software, you can actually automate some of the responses. For example, you could ask somebody for their hometown and their home state.

The email that's automatically written back to them thanking them for introducing themselves could include a fact about that state. For example, you might say, "How are things in Minnesota?" This can be automated, but it really feels personalized. To make things clearer, automation allows for personalization. Personalizing communications doesn't have to be manually written. Personalization can be scalable. What you do is think about how you would serve your ideal client if they were the only client you had. Think about that for a second. If you had only one client and that particular client was paying all of your bills, how would you adjust your communication and marketing efforts to serve them at a higher level? For example, if you wish that, when your ideal client opts in, they receive a personalized note, why don't you find a way to write a personalized note?

One of my clients has a monthly membership site. He discovered a lot of churn on his membership page i.e. a high number of people deciding not to continue with membership after a certain period of months. I suggested that he send a handwritten note to people that have been part of his membership site for a certain length of time. If, for example, most people drop off after Month Seven, then it makes sense that he would take just a few extra minutes to send a nice note during Month Six. Not only is this a cool feature, but it will also encourage people to stay an extra couple of months. This one action can provide necessary breakthrough contact that increases renewal rate and decreases churn.

For example, let's say my client charges $30 a month for his membership site and the average consumer drops off at 16 days. If that consumer was to stay just three extra months based on his hand written note to them, he would be up $90. The handwritten note is not worth $90. Furthermore, in our connected world of social media, it is very likely that people would take a picture of this note and post it on Twitter and on Instagram where it could serve as another form of marketing, thus adding new potential members. So, even if that member dropped off three months later but two new members opt-in, that one note is suddenly worth upwards of $500.

If this is the case, it follows that he should personalize these notes as much as possible. He's looking at a minor investment of time that will likely add to the social acclaim he'll receive as a result of additional personalization. Even if he finds himself with 1000 members, it is possible to skillet. He could have a team write a formal letter and then add personalized details, possibly signing each letter in his own handwriting. You get the idea.

Serving all as you would serve one.

That's the beauty of marketing automation: You can set up a system to serve everyone in your tribe the way you would serve your best customer. Because there's much that you can automate, try, and track, you can consistently be thinking of new ways to better serve your customer. These ways can then be automated and so the cycle continues.

When someone clicks your lead magnet, you want them to enter their first name and their email address. You might consider asking for even more after the initial opt-in. For example, you could offer the lead magnet with just a first name and email address. Then, on the next page, you can say, "Thank you, John. It's nice to meet you. What are your career goals that we might be able to help with?"

This is a great way to continue the momentum someone has provide by persuading them to take action. Once somebody enters information, they've already given you their trust, so it's likely that they are willing to continue the conversation. With the serum built into your WordPress site such as EntrePork, you can use one field on your site. This means you can pull in dynamic data onto your site to personalize the user experience. It's a really cool process.

Of course, if this is too complex or you ever need any help, you can contact us at the Dixon Agency. You might also consider a really basic opt-in such as MailChimp to start until you build your list and can afford a more complex tool.

Remember the mantra, "Hustle to the horizon." All you can do is be faithful with what's in front of you. Work as hard as you can on what is in front of you.

As you can see, there are several decisions that people must make to actually opt in.

Single versus double opt in:

A single opt-in is when someone enters their name and email once in exchange for your lead magnet. A double opt-in is when they enter their name and email and then have to click a confirmation link to confirm their interest in your offer. The reason for the confirmation link is that, in theory, someone can enter someone else's name and email address in an opt-in box, known as a false opt-in. Due to the fact that many people who opt-in and never click the confirmation email for a double opt-in, many email service providers are no longer requiring the confirmation of the opt-in and are now no longer requiring a double opt-in. Most of the major email marketing services are now allowing for a single opt-in.

Where to Put it and How it Works

The lead magnet chapter focuses on the offer. This chapter focuses on the transaction. Where do you put your opt-in?

For most websites, you should place your opt-in on the top right corner of your website. It should go "above the fold," which means that you should see it on the first page of your website. No scrolling required. You should also make sure that it fits the design of your website but stands out just enough for people to notice it.

Characteristics of a great Opt-In page

> Quick
> Simple
> Clean Design
> One Call to Action

An opt-in page or opt-in pop up should serve one main purpose: It is functional. The purpose of the opt-in page or opt-in pop up is for someone to enter their name and email and click "submit." That's it.

A Few Tips:

Don't Be Cutesy

Every once in a while I will see an opt-in page or pop up that doesn't use the standard "name, email, submit" format. Instead, they will use wording that feels like some kind of inside joke ("enter your codename here"). The problem with this is that most people won't get the joke. Inside jokes alienate anyone who isn't in on the joke, and that means losing out on possible opt-ins. Keep it simple, use plain language, and make it easy to opt-in.

Keep it Clear and Simple

Depending on the technology you use for your opt-in, it may allow for an "auto-fill", where "name" and "email" are already filled out in the box and, if it doesn't auto-fill the name and email, it might even say name and email inside the box already. When someone clicks the box, the indicated information disappears. If this is true, you'll need to indicate that name and email are required in the box. You never know how someone's browser will display those boxes.

Test Your Form on Multiple Devices

You never know exactly how your forms will appear on different screens, devices, and browsers. One great tip is to look at your website from multiple computers and multiple devices. My favorite tool for checking screen resolution and appearance is called ex.com.

Single Opt-In

Make entering your name and email simple and straightforward. Your system should be fast and it should give people immediate access to whatever they opted in for.

I highly recommend going for a single opt-in instead of a double opt-in. It is really annoying when you have to wait to access whatever you're opting in for. Instead of sending people to a confirmation page immediately, direct them to a page that delivers the thing that they opted in for. You want to give them what they asked for right away. I find that this process teaches your audience that taking action on your website is a rewarding process. I would much rather them get exactly what they're looking for and be happy than have them double opt-in and completely ignore the process.

One Call to Action

What do you want your website visitor to actually do? Give them one action to take. One clear "Call to Action". Your website should have one primary CTA (call to action). What do you want your website visitor to actually do? How you answer this question determines what your visitor's purpose is when they visit your page. Depending on your site and the content you already have, there may be many things you want people to do, but great websites don't make people think (credit to Steve Krug). Instead, great websites lead visitors down a clear path to follow. Your job is to make it very clear what you want your website visitor to do. For the majority of websites, and most likely yours, the best thing you can ask them to do is to exchange their name and email for your lead magnet.

As discussed in the previous chapter, a lead magnet builds trust. A lead magnet warms up your audience for your offering. A lead magnet builds credibility with your ideal audience. However, the best aspect of a lead magnet is that it helps you build a list of subscribers that you can offer a product to. Without a list of subscribers, you really have no business. Businesses do not exist without paying customers, and the best way to get paying customers online is to develop a subscriber list that you can regularly communicate with.

Opt-In tools

There are a few opt-in tools you might consider using. These include Landing Pages, Opt-in boxes, and Pop-up boxes.

Sidebar opt-in boxes

These are placed in the top right section of your website and allow website visitors to enter their name and email to download your free lead magnet. Most blogs have a "subscription box," which this opt-in box would replace.

Pop-up boxes

These are opt-in boxes the pop-up in front of the webpage content, requiring the visitor to either enter their information or close the pop-up box.

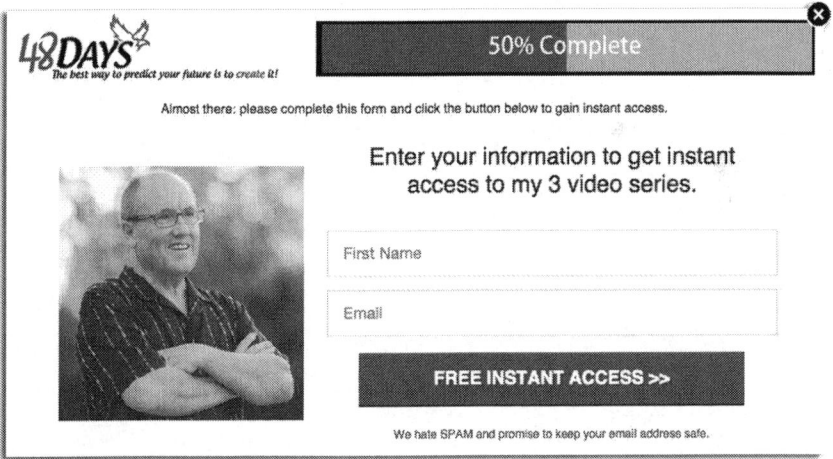

Figure 5: Here is an example of a pop-up opt-in box we created for Dan Miller. I especially like the clean design and branding that matches his website.

Landing pages

These are separate pages that offer the lead magnet in exchange for an opt-in. Since there is a whole page dedicated to the opt-in, there are several advantages to using a landing page instead of sidebar opt-ins or pop-up boxes. These include being able to show a video, share features and benefits, and track visitors with retargeting pixels.

My favorite tool for opt-in is called LeadPages. LeadPages is an online subscription service that allows you to create landing pages with opt-in forms. Although there are many lead page templates available that can virtually replace your website, the main purpose of LeadPages is to create opt-in forms.

Here's the basic process for working with Lead Pages:

One. Start with your opt-in first.

Start with your lead magnet first.

What do you want to offer to your potential subscribers? Depending on what your lead magnet is, you will choose a lead page template that's prebuilt to best sell the lead magnet.

For example, if you're offering a free webinar, you can use the webinar template from LeadPages that is already custom-built to present or sell the lead magnet. If you're offering a free PDF download, LeadPages even has a lead magnet delivery system built-in.

Two. Connect your mailing service.

Assuming you use MailChimp, you must work through the integrations and create a customized list in MailChimp that you can connect to this particular landing page. Anyone who fills out this particular form will automatically be added to that list and your MailChimp account. A really cool feature of LeadPages is that it automatically updates with all of your lists from MailChimp and other service providers. All you need to do is choose from a drop-down menu.

Now that you've chosen your template and connected your mailing program with the right mailing list, you need to customize your landing page. One key to using Lead Pages is to work within the template. It doesn't have to be complicated and it doesn't have to be fancy. The templates are already great as they are, but you may need to be a little creative in the way that you use the templates. For example, the headline of your landing page might only allow for two lines of text or a max of 240 characters, but your idea was to use more characters than that. Instead of trying to make a square peg fit into a round hole, my suggestion is that you customize your message according to LeadPages.

Every time I use LeadPages for a client, I have found that the best looking and best converting lead pages are the ones that stick to the template as closely as possible. You can find examples of our work at dixonagency.org, including the dozens of lead pages and landing pages we've customized for our clients.

Customizing your leadpage

When customizing your lead page, here are a few suggestions:

Vary the colors

Because LeadPages is a fairly popular program and the people that you're likely going to attract with your opt-in offer are fairly Internet savvy, the best thing you can do is make your page look like a customized page. Even though LeadPages makes it fairly easy, it's important for your brand to stand out in a crowded online marketplace. Everything you do should feel personalized; the message you're sending potential clients is that they will receive exceptional quality and exceptional service. What better way to say this than through an amazing first impression? Set the tone early on as we discussed in the first chapter.

For many of your new subscribers, your lead page will be their first impression of you. Before they see your cool business card, website, YouTube channel, Ted Talk, or whatever else, most will see your opt-in offer. Consequently, make your opt in page count. Customize the colors and fonts of your lead page. It will go a long way to saying you know what you're doing online; therefore, you are someone they can trust and someone who can help them accomplish their goals.

Writing headlines

Another tip for using LeadPages is customizing your headlines. Headlines are the main attention-getting words on your page. I have found that the best way for me to write headlines is to come up with many different examples and see what best fits the message and the design. To make it a truly streamlined experience, you want to make sure that the message comes across in a unified way.

Whenever you use templates, try to customize them. There are many services online now that allow you to buy stock photos or even pre-made logos. However, the brands that really stand out disguise the templates they use. They customize template work to fit their message and brand. Even if you're on a budget - which, let's face it, all of us are - you can still stand head and shoulders above the others out there because you take a little extra time to get it right.

Improve your images

For example, I recommend that, whenever my clients are launching a new product or program, they go with a professional photographer and get a new series of head shots. The reason I do this is because it makes a difference when you're reconnecting your tribe. Most of your customers will never meet you in person. That's part of the beauty of the Internet. So, all they know of you are the pictures they see on Facebook, your comments, and your blog.

When you change up your picture, it adds a little extra production value to say that you are someone who's a professional. So customizing your picture and using the color scheme from your photo shoot on your lead page can help you come up with a great design and also make an awesome brand impression on your potential subscribers.

Advanced tip

I would recommend checking out the templates on Lead Pages and come up with an archive or a swipe file. See content creator show episode 02X and use this swipe file as you plan your photo shoot. This way you'll know exactly what photos you need to take to get your brand across.

How to set up your first lead page

In this example video, I guide you step-by-step through the process using MailChimp.

Step 1. Research the topic. Find three places that someone has asked this question.

Step 2. Outline the process. Create a PDF checklist outlining a step-by-step process.

Step 3. Do a screenshot tutorial with screen grabs as you walk through the process.

Step 4. Edit the video in screenflow.

Step 5. Create the PDF checklist in InDesign5. Write the intro and the call to action.

Step 6. Film the intro and the call to action where you hold up the cheat sheet.

Step 7. Edit the video

Step 8. Upload the PDF. Place the PDF in your Ontraport account and grab the link.

Step 9. Paste the link onto the members' page.

The members' area would contain:

- A schedule of live tutorials; for example, we're going live now! Join us for the recording of this tutorial.
- Office hours
- Early access

- 10% discount
- Members' only bonuses

Pop-up boxes

To pop up or not to pop up?

Do you like pop-ups?

Most people say no. However, if you look at the website of any luminaries in your field, you'll notice that the majority use pop-ups. Do you know why? Because they work! Believe it or not, there are tasteful ways to use pop-ups on your page to encourage more people to opt-in to your list.

Delayed pop-up

A delayed pop-up appears 10 seconds or more after someone first visits your website. This gives them enough time to learn more about you. By this time, the visitor is ready to take action. If you time your pop up at the right interval, it shows up just before a visitor leaves your site. The best way to plan the timing of your delayed pop-up is to check your Google analytics accounts. This will give you detailed "time on site" information which you can use to perfectly time the pop-up's appearance.

Exit intent pop-up

One great way to use pop-ups is upon exit intent. This is when it is clear that a user is about to leave your website by scrolling over to the top menu bar. At that point, a pop-up appears with a customized message stating, "Don't leave empty-handed. Download my free checklist before you go." It is a really effective strategy.

First time only

Set your pop-up so that it only shows up the first time someone visits your website. You can then set a delay for 30 days so they won't see your pop-up again.

Opt-in technology

It's time to get technical. Once you have your lead magnet developed, such as a PDF, checklist, etc., you need to have the technology in place to complete the transaction. Here is what you will need to be able to accomplish this:

1. Collect the name and email address of your subscriber.
2. Automatically send the lead magnet to the subscriber.

You can do this in two ways. First, you can host the lead magnet on an opt-in page that you redirect to someone once they've confirmed their email address. Second, you can send an email to the subscriber that includes the PDF for them to download by clicking the link.

3. Now the new subscriber is added to an auto responder campaign where he receives a series of emails, building a relationship and proving the value of a future project or program you have to offer.
   In fact, the purpose of the lead magnet and the opt-in page is to turn a cold lead, a visitor who doesn't know you or trust you, through a sequential series of value-added content and warm them up to exchanging not just their email address but also their money for your valuable products or program.

Optimization

Ask yourself these questions to evaluate your opt-in page.

- How does the opt-in page convert?
- What is the conversion percentage of visitors to the lead magnet?
- Are the features and benefits of the lead magnet clear?
- Do your visitors readily exchange their information for the lead magnet on the opt-in page?

- Ensure the opt-in page includes a custom audience Facebook remarketing pixel to launch a retargeting campaign for interested prospects.

Methods to optimize your opt-in

Measuring conversions
    Benchmarking against your swipe file
    A/B testing (both lead magnets and opt-in pages)

AUTORESPONDER

Once someone signs up for your lead magnet, they are automatically entered into a series of emails called an email sequence that they will receive over the course of the next two weeks. Once a visitor becomes a subscriber, nurture them through a value-adding and educative email sequence which warms them for an eventual offer. The autoresponder will speak to the compelling needs and desires of the ideal prospect while informing them of the features and benefits you're offering. Your job is to measure opens, clicks, and unsubscribes throughout the campaign, and to continually revise the campaign based on these metrics.

How to Use Email to Nurture Your Prospects

When I have an initial Skype conversation consultation with a potential client, one of the first questions I ask him/her is about his/her email list. I want to know how many people have raised a hand and selected to receive updates from the potential client. Either you have an email or you don't. Use that as a Hatter.

It is your job to educate your customers. Your customers don't know that they need you and don't know how your services can help them. One of the best things that you can do is to educate them so that they are aware of how your services will help them reach their goal.

It's one simple question with only two possible answers: I don't have an email list or I have an

email list and here is the size. It's amazing how that one question alone can serve as a filter for those with whom we work at the Dixon Agency. The reason for that is simple: The correct answer is, " I have an email list and this is the size." Without a list, you don't have a business. Your email list is made up of contact information for people who have told you that they want to engage in your content. If you don't have anyone who has said, "Yes, I want to engage in your content", you don't really have a business. Instead, you have an idea.

It might be a great idea. It might be the best idea anyone has ever had, and it should make you millions and millions of dollars. However, without an email list, who is going to hear about your idea? You'll have to find other ways to put your information in front of these wonderful people who are going to buy your stuff. You have to pay to get it in front of them. You have to get other people to sing your praises to everyone and tell them about how awesome your stuff is.

All of that being said, the best thing that you can do to grow your business online is to increase the number of people on your email list. This is the essence of the FLOATS model and why we start with the lead magnet to entice people to get on your email list. When someone is on your list, you have the opportunity to nurture them. That is all you have: "opportunity."

Now let's talk about the process.

When someone enters their name and email to download your lead magnet, that contact information is automatically entered through a form into your email marketing platform. If you set it up in the right way, which we'll talk about in this chapter, then you have added that person to a specific list and they received some marking characteristics, known as tags, based on where they came from, what they subscribed to, what their other behavior on the website has been so far, and any demographic information your system might be able to pick up along the way.

Once they're automatically entered into the system, they usually receive an email confirmation. This is called a double opt in. Opting in is the process of raising your hand and saying, "Yes, I want to receive more information." In theory, someone else could've filled out the online form with someone else's name and email. For this reason, many email service providers require a double opt in. All this means is that the prospect would get a prewritten email saying, "Click here to confirm your interest in this email list."

Once they click, they are officially added to your list. In the meantime, they're added to a bit of an email Purgatory, a holding cell while the system waits for them to opt in by clicking. If they never click that email confirmation, they will never be added to your list. It's as simple as that.

Once they're added to your list, you should have a sequence of emails that are automatically sent out. The reason that you have a sequence of emails, is that it takes time to build a relationship and you want to lay the ground rules for that relationship. Because people will subscribe on the weekend, or at 2 o'clock in the morning, or while you're on vacation, you want to have automatic responders, known as autoresponders, that systematically respond to a person's request for more information during the first week or two.

These are new prospects, and they need nurturing. Just like a newborn baby, they don't have any idea what to do. But they're here and that's enough. It's your job to build a relationship with them. The way you do this is through sending out 3 to 5 emails, automatically, over the course of the first week and a half, letting them know that signing up for your email list was a really good idea. If you don't provide high-quality, valuable content through your emails, then after the first two or three, people will unsubscribe or be trained to ignore all future emails. You want to avoid that.

You can do this by making sure that those first initial emails are packed with valuable content. If you subtly train visitors to read your emails regularly, they will learn to expect value from you every time they open up a message from you. Your goal is to give visitors even more value. Once they sign up for your email list, look for ways to build an even deeper relationship by establishing that you're someone who is going to give valuable stuff away for free. If your free stuff is this good, imagine how valuable your paid stuff will be!

Once somebody signs up for your lead magnet, make sure that the emails that he/she automatically receives are packed with valuable content. The goal of the first few emails is to train someone to read your emails. The way to do that is to make sure that the content is valuable enough for them to expect value every time they open up your email.

What should I say?

Emails should come across as personal. You want to enter the conversation that your prospect is already having in his or her own mind. The best emails are ones that are written for the benefit of the subscriber and not for your own benefit. You want to balance content, personality, and personal connections. From studying some of the best marketers out there, I have found that most will invite prospective clients into their lives. Of course, much of this invitation is on the surface level, but it's more personal an interaction than people are used to receiving from the average business.

How to setup an autoresponder

Here's how to setup an autoresponder.

1. Write the emails
2. Schedule the email
3. Create opt-out rules

For example, a well-known blogger recently sent out an email with the subject line, "Pink or Blue?" Notice how that subject line does not say, "Get 50% off for my new program." Instead, it's a subject line that gets you to open the email. It also gets you wondering, "What is he talking about?" It piques your curiosity. In fact, even though I knew that this email was from a marketer and that he was launching a program that I was not planning on buying, I still wanted to open up the email just to see what it was talking about. I guessed that it had something to do with having a baby and figuring out whether it was a boy or a girl.

And sure enough, when I opened it up it said that he and his wife were pregnant and finding out the gender of the baby that day. He then went on to explain his excitement about his new program that was launching and related it to the excitement that he was feeling for the birth of his new child.

I know what you're thinking, a bit of a stretch, right? Well, honestly, I was expecting it to feel like a stretch, but it really didn't. It was coming from the heart of a proud first-time dad. This particular marketer was savvy enough to use psychological triggers to elicit emotion and get people to take action; he did it masterfully.

Another well-known marketer shared in many emails, podcasts, and even some live webinars that she was upgrading her lifestyle by moving from from her post-college, two-bedroom condo to her dream home overlooking the water in sunny Southern California. Instead of this communication feeling braggadocious, (i.e. if only we listen to her wise words we might have a shot at being hugely successful too), it felt like she was opening up and sharing an important part of her life.

She found effective ways to make a connection between the anticipation of purchasing a new home and embracing change, and the expectation one might feel when upgrading his/her life by seeking out further training and purchasing tools that help in accomplishing more. Her emails were really saying, "Change is normal. You're going to experience resistance to change. I am experiencing resistance to change, but I know what it's like to struggle and I know what it's like to succeed. I am someone from whom you can learn. Trust me. When you buy my program, you're not just buying content, you're getting access to a real person who knows what it's like to be you. A person who understands what it's like to walk in your shoes."

Do you see the genius of that email strategy? Yours needs to be similar. Imagine you've been doing this online business for a while when someone you've always admired from a distance, but never truly connected with, suddenly signs up for your email newsletter. What are you going to say to him? Are you so proud of your emails and the personality that comes through that you wouldn't change a thing? What about a person in your field whom you really respect? That famous speaker or author or TV personality. What if she subscribed to your email? Would you make any changes? If so, I challenge you to make those changes right now. An email responder or auto responder campaign should be written for that person, that someone you deeply admire and greatly respect. Somebody you would love to convert from a visitor, to a subscriber, to a customer.

How the system works

When you think about email in this context it's not like your traditional email from Outlook or Gmail or Hotmail. You're not actually logging in to your email program and sending out individual messages. Instead, it's more like a newsletter. You have serialized content - episode one, episode two, episode three, or in this case, email one, email two, and email three, which are being sent out sequentially. Your subscribers would get the first email, then a few days later they'd get the second email, and so on.

Building a relationship

The purpose of the autoresponder sequence is to continue building a relationship that transforms the subscriber into a customer. Keep in mind that with these emails, you are teaching and training recipients to become ideal customers. As you design your email autoresponder sequence, consider what would make someone the perfect customer for your product.

- What do they need to know?
- What do they need to believe?
- What do they need to have ready?

Your autoresponder sequence

When developing your autoresponder sequence, consider how you can serve your ideal audience. Like everything else, the autoresponder sequence should be filled with value, so always be thinking about how you can add even more. This series of emails is your chance to educate the subscribers you want most. Remember, once they opt in for your lead magnet, they'll automatically be added to your email sequence, so let's walk through an example sequence:

0. Offer of free lead magnet
1. Here is your lead magnet
2. Little known secret
3. A solution for you, name
4. Three reasons you shouldn't
6. Almost gone (last email)
7. Convert to newsletter

Remember: if you already have an email list, you can use a teaser email to reengage your list by offering them something valuable.

Example Email Zero

subject: How to get your first coaching client [pdf]

Name, so you're just getting started as a coach – Congratulations!

Coaching is a rewarding business and can open the door for your personal, professional, and financial growth.

Regardless of the industry, building a base of loyal clientele can be a difficult process. No matter how good you are as a coach, if you sit around and wait for word-of-mouth (or luck) to bring you your first client, you may be sitting for a long time.

Don't let that get you down - you can break into the coaching arena by being creative. I've put together a list of my 10 Tips for Getting Your First Coaching Client. These are tried, reliable practices you can begin using today. If you're ready to get started, click here:

http://www.48days.com/clients

Stay inspired,
Dan

EMAIL ONE: Here is your lead magnet

The first email actually delivers the lead magnet that somebody opted in for. If they opted in for a video course, this might be their username and password to access the concept.

You might also include an attachment to this email or, preferably, a link that he/she can click to download the content. If you're using a CRM you'll want to track this.

In your first email, delivering your lead magnet, you want to have a brief reminder about why somebody signed up and what can be expected from you. At this point, he/she is a hot prospect. Action has just been taken which might result quickly in more action, so consider going for the sale in this email. Depending on what you have to offer, you might ask them to join your community or to leave some sort of feedback. **#write more? Brian, did I read this correctly, a person might want to go for the sale in this email? Just checking….**

Example Email One:

Name, thanks for your interest in my free PDF:

10 Tips for Getting Your First Coaching Client.

I'm excited to be part of launching (or building) your coaching business.

Click here to download the PDF.

Make sure you check out tip #5 – it can mean the difference between casual and career coaching.

Thank you for being part of the 48Days community.

Stay inspired,
Dan

EMAIL TWO: A little known industry secret

The second email your subscribers will receive is your best tip or inside information. That's right. Don't hold anything back. This is the first email in a sequence of emails to build trust and credibility. Gently sell your subscriber on becoming a customer. Whispering some insider industry information to your new subscriber is one of the best ways for you to build trust and credibility in his/her eyes.

So what kind of secret do I write about, exactly? Great question. Since you know your industry well, you know that there are certain false assumptions or myths that are out there. These beliefs are usually what separates the beginner from the expert. In the first email tell the sequence secret to shorten the learning curve of your subscriber by telling him/her what mindset shift is needed to master the industry. Another subject line you can use for this email is "the hard truth about…you fill in the blank." This email establishes you as someone who is not afraid to tell the truth about your industry. Although the very nature of sending an email implies that you want something from the subscriber, you can distract readers from this underlying need by proving that you're passing along valuable, actionable teaching.

In Parker's example, the subject line of his first email could be about cold calling. In his industry he has, no doubt, discovered certain truths about cold calling. For example, he might've experienced the fact that it takes 27 cold calls to find one warmed-up prospect. What Parker knows is that every beginner wants a shortcut to success. No beginner wants to make the 27 calls it takes to get to that one ideal prospect.

But Parker knows from his years of experience that it's a basic numbers game. If there are 3000 people on your calling list, 100 of them are likely ready to make a decision about your product. Everyone else is either too busy, satisfied with their current product or the status quo, doesn't have the budget, or does not have the authority to make the decision.

A beginner might say this list is bad, but Parker knows if there's just one diamond in a list of 3000, the list is good. It takes consistent discipline and follow-through to reach that one diamond. This is the essence of the sales industry - the little known secret is that the person who wins is the one who does the most work. Throughout the email campaign, Parker will share other additional secrets and other more advanced tips, but the best thing he can say is that it's a lot of hard work with a lot of hung up phone calls.

So his first email could have one of the following subject lines:

- The truth about cold calling
- What you didn't know about cold calling
- Cold calling secrets
- I too, was surprised by the stats
- How many times?
- That can't be true
- One out of 27

The purpose of the email subject line is to get someone to read the email. That's it. As you can see from the example above, some of the subject lines pique curiosity more than they inform what the email is about. And that is okay. A great email helps you enter the conversation your prospects are already having in their minds. Think about the user psychology. They just signed up for your lead magnet, helping them master the art of telephone sales. They downloaded your checklist and spent a few minutes looking at it, but they are overwhelmed and likely need a coach to help them truly be successful in their direct sales efforts. The next day they get an email from you telling them "the truth about cold calling." Not only is this email timely, it's also relevant.

EMAIL THREE: "A solution for you, [Name]."

Given the fact that your last email just exposed an industry secret and you've established yourself as someone who tells the truth no matter how difficult, the next email is going to give them some help. The next email introduces a solution to the problem they read about in the last email. For example, with Parker, the problem is that most people do not make the 27 phone calls necessary to get to the one ideal prospect. They get discouraged, they want to give up, so they don't make that necessary number of phone calls. A solution would be a better way. There is a better way to cold call; there is a better way to stay motivated when pounding through 27 no's in search of that one yes.

I like using email three to help show how joining my client's program can help the reader FINALLY get results. Others have called these emails "results in advance." You want the reader to believe that when he/she invests in the program a much needed breakthrough will be experienced. Often, this email is where I see a sales bump.

Example Email Three

Subject: Are you in the top 5%? You could be…

Coaches typically make between $40 and $200 an hour. Why is it, then, that 95% of coaches never make more than $40,000 a year?

One reason is this: these people aren't making the best use of their content. Once you understand the concepts of re-purposing your content, you can see how $100,000 a year is not unreasonable.

Coaching with Excellence LIVE will clearly outline the "business side" of coaching, illuminating the different ways you can leverage your content and ultimately maximize your coaching income.

Here's what you'll learn at Coaching with Excellence:

— What is a coach? Why is coaching growing in popularity…and am I cut out to be one?

- How to create and/or build your coaching business
- Sales and marketing strategies to build your business funnel
- Facilitating client and business relationships for win/wins
- Plus….a bonus offer for the Coaching Mastery Program, exclusive to CWE Grads!

At <u>Coaching With Excellence</u>, you'll also receive resources amounting to more than $450 in value. They'll include:

- Coaching Business Basics
- Overview of Coaching Trends and the Current Coaching Business Practices
- 25+ page Personality Profile
- Coaching Starter Kit reference guide book
- Marketing Plan for Filling Your Schedule
- 8 Methods of Generating Additional Income
- Strategic plan for recapturing your full investment with your first client
- Catered meals with the 48 Days Team
- Plus bonus items!

The benefits are many, the reasons not to come…?
Well, we can't think of any. We look forward to seeing you here.
<u>Click here to join us for Coaching with Excellence</u>.

Stay Inspired,
Dan

EMAIL FOUR: Customer testimonial

This fourth email allows you to brag about the results your subscriber could get by joining your program, without sounding like you are bragging about them yourself. Let your customers do the bragging for you.

Example Email Four

subject: "one of the best investments I've ever made"

Name, are you interested in taking your coaching business to the next level?

Coaching with Excellence LIVE is an exciting two-day experience focused on exploring what is happening right now in the coaching world and how you can get in the game!

If you've been a member of the 48Days community for a while, you know that I love to celebrate the success of others. I'm proud and excited to say that Coaching with Excellence LIVE has helped spur on the success of some truly gifted individuals. One such individual is Jevonnah Ellison – here's what she has to say about Coaching with Excellence LIVE:

"I attended Coaching with Excellence and also joined Coaching Mastery. Having Dan as my coach has been a game changer in my business and he has proven over and over again to be one of the best investments I've ever made. He encourages, challenges, and inspires me to great heights like never before. My coaching business is exploding and I owe so much of that growth to Dan for being an extraordinary leader and coach. So if you're thinking about going to Coaching with Excellence in 2015, take action. If you're willing to put the time and effort in, Dan has the wealth of knowledge, experience and wisdom to guide you along the way."

While extraordinary, Jevonnah's growth is not unique. We have seen exceptional improvement in many others who have joined us at Coaching with Excellence Live.

How would you like to live your own success story? Click here to join us for Coaching with Excellence.

Stay Inspired,
Dan

EMAIL FIVE: Almost gone (last email)

This last email delivers an ultimatum. Ideally, there is an authentic deadline your subscriber must meet. The program is closing tonight. The conference is starting in just two weeks and people have to book flights. Give them a reason to take action NOW or else they will miss out.

Example Email Five:

subject: Almost full... but we are missing YOU!

Name, we only have a few spots left for the May 21-22, 2015 Coaching With Excellence LIVE event until we are completely SOLD OUT.

I would love to see you join us, so act now and click here to register.

Stay Inspired,
Dan

EMAIL SIX: Convert to newsletter
So what makes a great email?

Every email you send should be a great email. Think about it, if you were building a list of 10,000 people, you want to write an email that's worthy of 10,000 people opening and reading it. Two characteristics of a quality email are solid teaching and a clear call to action.

Solid teaching

Every single email you send should teach your reader something. By teaching in your emails, you are training your subscribers to open your emails and expect value. In a world of constant overwhelming choices and sales pitches, you can be the person who cuts through the clutter because every time you send an email there is something valuable your subscribers are going to get. What kind of valuable things can you send? Favorite links, favorite resources, tips, tricks, shortcuts, affiliates, training resources, podcast episodes, blog post links - things like that.

Respect the inbox

Here's an important new rule: respect the email inbox. With so many spammers out there, you can set yourself apart by respecting your subscribers' email inbox. Become the person who clearly puts a lot of time into the emails that you send, making them so good that you are hard to ignore. Now that individuals have visited your website, opted in and downloaded your lead magnet, and received a confirmation email, you need to permanently convince them that your emails are worth opening because of the value you can offer. The best way to do this is to make sure that every email is worth opening. That's worth repeating: every email you send to your subscribers should be worth opening. Every email delivers massive value, engaging content, and actionable teaching.

Developing a swipe file

As you surf about on the Internet you should keep a swipe file or a list of resources you want to share with your audience. Assume that a cool trick that you just discovered is one your subscribers have never heard of before. You can be the first one to tell them about it. For example, I love using the app Scrivener. Even though I've been using Scrivener for three or four years, most people in my audience have never used it themselves, and some have never even heard of it.

So an easy email promotion would sound something like this:

"By the way, I wrote my e-book using my favorite writing app called Scrivener. If you've never heard about it, you need to check it out here; it's really good!" Notice how this doesn't come across as "salesy" at all, but actually value adding? You can even include an affiliate link while adding value. It truly is a new world out there.

Working through the sequence

If your eventual sale is for a toolkit, then each of your emails should give away part of the toolkit. For example, if your toolkit helps people hire, then parts of your toolkit should talk about what to look for in an ideal employee.

This would be the subject line of one of the emails:

"Here is what you need to look for in an ideal employee."

That's a great way to start the conversation and build a relationship.

TEASING THE OFFER

By the way selling
Trust and credibility must be built first. Then, the offer is made in a "by the way" fashion. If you like my free stuff, you'll love my paid stuff. By the way, I have a new program opening on Tuesday. I'd love you to join the community.

It's like a party invite. Subtle. Exclusive. Intriguing.

Selling "by the way"
The best sales happen in the postscript. By the way, my program x is closing soon. To learn more click here.
Testimonial (our friend Bryce)
Did you know?
My x is closing soon
This is your last chance

Tease the offer - generate top of mind awareness by staying in front of the prospects by using emotional triggers including social proof, scarcity, and perceived value.

- Include these messages in the postscript of the auto responder campaign
- Remarket to prospects through social media custom audience tracking

People love to buy, but hate to be sold; that is why we tease the offer. Ideally, you're presenting a "choose your own adventure" strategy. The subscribers are only presented with a choice when they're ready for it. In a choose your own adventure book, you have a choice between entering the door or going down the hallway. It's either/or.

After someone has opted in, they receive a series of autoresponders, which are scheduled emails that go out at specific intervals to help nurture the relationship. Throughout these emails, you want to drop small hints about your upcoming product or program. We call these hints "teasing the offer."

How do you move the conversation from, "I like this guy and I learned a lot from him," to, "I want to give him money?" That's what teasing the offer is all about - a subtle shift in the relationship from engaging the reader to creating a purchasing customer.

Instead of advertising and going for the hard-sell based on price or scarcity or social proof, you are encouraging your subscribers to buy based on value, not just based on the deal they can score. This is significant given the prices you can charge in the content marketing world are astronomical compared to what you might charge in retail.

This is where the sale takes place. Sales today are made through hints. We know this from dating. You never want to say, "Hey, I really like you and I would like you to ask me on a date!"

Instead you drop hints. You wear a new shirt or you intentionally sit next to someone. You make these efforts with the idea that eventually the other person will pick up on the hints that you're dropping. When the effort doesn't work out, even though you are disappointed, you realize that the other person wasn't for you anyway.

Retargeting and Facebook pixels

Once someone has hit your website, you want to display your offer wherever you can. An advanced strategy you can use for this is called retargeting. Retargeting is a way for you to re-engage someone who's been to your website. By installing a small snippet of code on your website you can run ads that only target those visitors who have already been to your site.

Teasing the offer by nurturing

Once prospects have raised their hands and moved from a visitor to a subscriber, it's time to nurture that relationship and move them into becoming your customers. We know that people buy from those who they know, like, and trust, and when building the rapport required for that exchange of money, you need to nurture your subscribers. Nurturing your subscribers is done by consistently providing value that positions your content and all of your messages as something worth paying attention to.

Your goal

A thriving business starts and ends with serving your customer, and the best way to serve your customer in the online world is to provide exclusive, creative, high-value, actionable content that inspires, instructs, informs, and enables him or her to achieve goals.

So how do you build that nurturing relationship? The answer is simply, time. Relationships are built over time and shared experiences. This is true for our friendships, our dating relationships, and it is just as true for our customers. Instead of thinking about marketing to your subscribers, think about building a relationship. Remember, people buy from those whom they know, like, and trust.

A proven method of teasing the offer:

1. Send valuable email messages that people open.
2. Use the PS post script of the emails to mention offhand that there is an offer available if they're interested.
3. Present the offer as a side conversation.

For those who have done it effectively, and of course I mean people like Amy Porterfield, Brendon Burchard, Eben Pagan, and Michael Hyatt, it feels very much like a side conversation. For example, my wife Julie and I were at a Christmas party, and I was engaged in an interesting conversation, and she leaned over and tapped me on the shoulder. Now I know that that meant she was ready to leave. I gave her a knowing nod and continued with my conversation. When situations like this occur, and I don't actually leave in the next three or five minutes I might get another subtle hint like Julie handing me my coat or the keys or she might enter the conversation to say, "It was really great to meet all of you. Thanks again for having us over." The really effective communication is happening in the background, something that only she and I understand. A gesture, a glance, a signal. It's our secret code.

Paying my way through graduate school, I found that going to garage sales to buy items for a dollar or two and selling them on Amazon or eBay for five or six dollars was a great way to make some extra income. I actually learned the secret of garage sales from my mother and father, who have thriving Amazon and eBay side businesses. Whenever I was at a garage sale with my mom and she was asking if something she was holding was worth purchasing for sale on eBay or Amazon, she would ask, "Do you think Uncle Ernie would like this?"

It was our secret code. It was a lot better than saying in front of the people running the garage sale, "Do you think these people are suckers, and we can get a good enough price to buy this item, turn around and sell it later today, for four or five times what we paid?" Instead, she simply asked, "Do you think Uncle Ernie would like this?"

Now, the best part is that instead of saying, "No, I do not think that we can make a profit off of that item," I could just say, "I don't think it's the right size." Or, "It's not his favorite color." Or, "I think he already has too many of those." And honestly, it didn't even matter what I said; the point was I didn't give a thumbs up or thumbs down. My mom was just looking for somebody to give her some feedback before making the buying decision. Our secret code is what made it an experience.

Every communication, every YouTube video, every Facebook post, every email autoresponder, is your opportunity to build a secret language and a secret code with your audience. It is your chance to say, "You know that goal you've been working towards? Well, I've got a little something for you."

Down in Louisiana where we lived for several years, they call this "lagniappe," and it simply means a little something extra. This email is going to provide a bunch of value to you and teach you something very specific. The email itself will stand on its own. But the P.S. takes it to the next level - example: If you want a little something extra you need to check this out over here.

That's all it is.

Teasing the offer is a subtle way of communicating that your insiders will understand. The point is to prompt them to click on the link which will lead them to a sales pitch. Once you get them to the sales page, then you go for the hard sell. The sales page is the moment when you're down on your knee with the ring box open, tearing up in the eyes, and asking a question. But before you have that opportunity, you need to set up the situation. We set up a situation by nurturing the relationship through autoresponders that train your subscribers to believe you are someone worth buying from. And then you tease the offer. You make subtle hints to say, "What kind of ring do you like?" " Have you ever thought about getting married at a large church?" "How many kids would you like to have one day?"

An ongoing conversation in the background helps to define the relationship. Not the main conversation, but a side conversation teasing the offer. A little something extra. This, right here, is the secret to growing my business. I couldn't believe it myself, but this has made all the difference. See how that works? You just read a valuable email with some great training, and all of a sudden there's a suggestion. Wouldn't you want to follow a suggestion from somebody who just gave you something really valuable? That is how teasing the offer works.

Did you know?
My x is closing soon
    Postscript Examples
    Testimonial (our friend Bryce)
    This is your last chance.

SALES PAGE

The most important phase of FLOATS is the sales page. You could have great rapport with your audience. You could have an offer; you could have an awesome product. But if your sales page is not efficient, you will miss out on the reward everyone who started an online business seeks out - to actually make some money! The sales page is where you finally present your offer. And there are multiple strategies when it comes to building a sales page that actually makes sales.

The jargon

Before we dive into the elements of a sales page, here are a few keywords you need to know:

Conversion rate

The conversion rate is the percentage of visitors who become buyers. For example, if you had 100 visitors to your sales page and seven people purchased your product, your conversion rate is 7%.

A swipe file

A swipe file is a repository of best practices. These are screenshots of sales pages that you've taken all over the web - at your desktop, laptop, and mobile - sales pages that actually get people to buy. One of the best practices you can adopt is to develop a swipe file capture system. As someone who has something to say and something to sell online, you want to develop a place to capture the best ideas you see online. Developing a swipe file prevents you from having to reinvent the wheel every time you want to launch a new product. Since we work with many clients across multiple industries, we have developed a group swipe file. As a full-time Internet marketer, whenever I find a sales page that motivates me to take out my credit card or enter my PayPal password, I know they did something right. I take a screenshot of the sales page and save it in a folder on a Dropbox account.

Once a prospect has decided to become a customer, remove any barriers to entry. Evaluate the sales page to make it as easy as possible for the customer to "buy."

- Test and improve the checkout process.
- Offer a clear roadmap explaining the onboarding sequence
- Test every element on this page to maximize conversions

Once you've warmed up your subscribers, tease them into letting them know what you're actually selling to make the sale. The sales page is your place to present your offer to your subscribers. In this chapter we're going to walk through the elements of an effective online sales page, talk about pricing, learn about the technology you need to deliver the content, share examples of compelling sales pages, and share with you a few innovative ways to launch products.

Minimum viable product

What is the least amount of work you need to do to test if a product is going to sell? One of the mistakes I see people new to online business make is fully creating a product before they have tested to see if the market would like that product. Instead I recommend that you develop a "minimum viable product". This term, coined by Tim Ferriss in The Four Hour Work Week, is the least amount you need to invest in a product to find out if your customers would actually purchase it.

So for example, instead of writing, shooting, editing, and producing a 12 part online video course before you to try sell it, test it out. Create a simple sales page and make the offer. If people try to purchase your course, send them to a page that says the product is still in development and offer them a discount on the future product in exchange for their name and email. Implementing a minimum viable product strategy can save you countless hours of product development working on a course that no one really wants.

This is a great strategy for authors. Instead of spending countless hours writing 12 chapters of your book, just focus on writing the best single chapter you can. Offer this chapter as your free lead magnet and offer the rest of the book as a preorder for your upsell. You can even take payment as long as you clearly communicate that the book is still in preorder status and won't be available until a specific date.

Split testing

Once you have even a small bit of traffic, you can conduct a split test. A split test is where a percentage of your audience sees one version, version A, of your sales page and another percentage sees version B. The results are then tracked and you can make a decision as to which of the sales pages should be shown more often.

Generally, a good split test focuses on only one variable at a time. For example, you might test a sales page with a video and then without a video. Or change the text on your sales page, otherwise known as the copy, from one headline to another headline. These are different ways to split test.

How to develop new products

There are three ways to develop new products:

- Ask your audience
- Test a new idea
- Answer a question

These are three effective ways to create new products. The first is to ask your audience. If you know exactly who you're meant to serve, you can just ask them, "What would you like to buy? What products or program would help you achieve your goal?" Most of the time your audience will already know. Ideally, you can even build a customer list of people who are interested in the product you're developing. If you have a list of 100 or more people, and you ask them what kind of product they would like to see developed, and 20 say that they would like to see a specific product, you can now create a sales page and send it directly to those 20 people, inviting them to purchase. You can even split test a page on a small group to see the results before you launch the page to a larger group of people.

When you have a truly original idea

One of the rebuttals to the survey strategy is an old Henry Ford quote. He talks about how there's one caveat to asking your audience about product development, and it is applicable when the product you're creating is brand-new. You know that your audience won't understand exactly how they can use the product without some nurturing. Asking an audience about a new strategy, or even a new technology, before they're ready for it will give you a false negative result. They won't be interested in the product without more information. This applies to Henry Ford's quote, "If I asked my audience what they wanted, they would've asked for faster horses." Of course, Henry Ford developed the first mass-market automobile, so it just goes to prove that his audience wasn't ready to ask for a car. They didn't really understand the concept at that point. So if you're developing something new, surveying your audience might not be the best method of discovering a new product to create.

Integrate your survey with your CRM

When you survey your audience, consider ways to include the results or consider ways to include andor import the results into your customer relationship management (CRM) software. A survey is a great way to round out the data in your CRM. Including your customer's mailing address, age, any demographic information, and definitely information about their business and the life cycle of their business, can help you develop better products in the future and serve them at a higher level.

Video overview

A video overview is a compelling way to draw in your subscribers and present your offer to them. Generally a video overview is a form of welcome and includes the following:

One. Text on screen

This video overview can simply be a presentation created in PowerPoint and narrated into the computer's microphone. The video overview is your sales video where you explain who the product is for, what the product features, how these features help customers achieve their goals, and also allows you to include any credibility statements. A credibility statement lets people know that they are not taking a risk on this product because it has been proven to work for people like them. In the overview video you present your product, and you include the pricing details. Now, there's a psychology to creating an effective sales video and the best practices for delivering a sales video are constantly being developed.

With so many options available, so many people teaching best practices, and best practices continually changing, you need to remember that it is very common to get lost in the world of new information. Of course, there is value for learning what works and applying it to your business. But it is much better to apply a technique to your business than to continually discover whatever the new technique happens to be.

As a quick example, I had a membership to all of the online videos from a marketing conference a few years ago. In total there were 26 videos covering everything from sales funnels to email marketing to Facebook ads. Six months later, I received an email offering the videos from the most recent conference and again, there were about 26 videos. Instead of purchasing access to all those new videos, what I should have done was wait until I'd applied everything I'd learned from the first round.

I challenge you to do the same. Use the tools you have to their fullest capacity. Do the work with what you have and upgrade later. Strong implementation with reliable material can work better than always reaching for new ideas.

Sales video

You can outsource the production of your sales video to someone on fiverrr.com for a fairly low investment. At the writing of this book I found several listings on fiverrr from people willing to create explainer videos, write sales copy, and do professional voice-over narration. You can hire someone to do all of this for five dollars each. Which means that for only $15 or $25 you could have a sales video done in the next couple of days. My favorite kind of sales video is one where we can actually see you, or a "talking head video." It's you, your face, on the screen introducing yourself and explaining what you have for sale.

We truly live in a world of no excuses. As long as you have a computer with Internet access, you can do almost anything. You can read almost anything, watch almost anything, create almost anything, buy almost anything, and sell almost anything. Excuses are no longer valid. No one cares who your parents are or what your last name is, where you live, if you have an accent or what the color of your skin is. You can make money online selling products that meet a need.

We don't have the space in this book to talk about affiliate products and white label sales, but just know that it is possible for you to sell products without having to make anything. I personally know people who are making over $1 million a year simply offering links for people to click on. They have built up a targeted audience that needs their services. So there are no more excuses. Our world is too full of opportunities.

Elements of the Sales Page

There are certain elements you need to create a sales page.

- Showcase the features and benefits of the product.
- Include a clickable button to buy the product. That clickable button leads to a checkout process, which can lead people to your shopping cart, to a PayPal checkout, or to a form to fill out to buy and download your product.
- If you're just starting out, you might even send people to an external store such as an Etsy store, Amazon, or eBay.

Here is the system that we use with our clients and that I would recommend to you: build the sales page in LeadPages.

- This allows you to A-B test the sales page
- This allows you to insert a Facebook custom audience pixel to read target visitors to your sales page
- This allows you to create a custom exit intent pop up for your sales page
- This creates mobile and responsive ready sales pages proven to work
- Upload your product to your shopping cart system
- We use Ontraport for our shopping cart, but others have recommended Zen Cart, Foxycart, Big Commerce, and others.
- Include the digital file or email instructions for accessing the contacts.
- Create a checkout page
- Create a custom header image for the checkout page to unify the user experience with similar logo, color scheme, and fonts.

So what should you put on your sales page? In this section, I'll walk you through each of the elements of an effective sales page and provide you with examples of each of these. Take a page to break each one of these down and give examples:

Overview video

Outline of the program

Testimonials

Features

Benefits

Clear results

Clear contents

Guarantee

Clear audience

Clear value

Clear offer

Call to action

Through the entire FLOATS process you are leading people to a sales page. Once they click on the sales page there are certain proven elements you want present on your page to convert them from viewers to customers.

Sales pages and their design are constantly changing. There really is no one way to create a sales pitch. I've seen sales pages which were a simple video and a button with a place to enter a credit card number. I've also seen sales pages that run on for 20 or more screens with dozens of testimonial features and benefits, but for the most part, the basic elements of a good sales page are covered in this section. The key takeaway is to build it, launch it, test, and improve it. Until you launch, you won't know if it's working.

110 | Online Sales Formula

Figure 6: This sales page we created for Dan Miller features a countdown timer and two package options.

Overview video

In my opinion the most important element of the sales page is an overview video. An overview video introduces you, introduces the offer, and makes the pitch. It covers everything that you would have on a sales page in one compact container. Some of my favorite sales pages only include a video. Video still has a novelty factor which I'm pretty sure will never wear off because there's nothing quite as personal as video on the Internet. You get to see the person's face, you get to hear a voice, you get to notice body language and the setting. It gives you the best glimpse of who you're going into business with and if you can trust them. No text can replace that. So all of my sales pages start with a video.

Here are a few best practices:

- The video should autoplay
  Videos on the sales page should autoplay, which means that once your site is done loading, the video starts to play. I like to add a few seconds of music and a personal story at the beginning of the video. This draws the viewer in to learn a little bit more about you and what you have to offer. It's hard to stop a video once it's started until you know what a person is talking about. If you put yourself in the mindset of the person visiting your website he/she is there and now they are watching your video. They found your site, you have their attention, so make a video to explain what you have to offer that will benefit them.
- Production quality
  Video can be a black hole when it comes to investment in quality. In fact, I've never seen someone hit the ceiling of what we know is possible when it comes to video. Even the latest, coolest multimillion dollar blockbuster hit can still take production value to the next level. You can always add animation, graphics, and other elements

to show that you truly are an expert. **So be careful not to chase that moving target of video quality.** The answer to the question of how good should my video be, is simply, good enough to make the sale. That's it. Your video should be good enough to make the sale. If you were selling a $2,000 program, the video should feel like it's part of a $2,000 program. This would include microphone, lighting, scripts, wardrobe, delivery, and quality.

I would argue that even if you're selling a $17 program, the video should be good. You can never go wrong by improving the quality of your sales video. The only place you can make a mistake here is by taking so much time on the quality that you never actually launch the video. So if you have to choose between complete and perfect, always choose complete. You can always reinvest and can always improve later. Focus on getting it done and then on improving it. Remember the adage, "Ask him never to compare your beginning to someone else's middle." It's important to shoot high and to make sure that the quality is there, but don't let that stop you from finishing. Finishing makes all the difference.

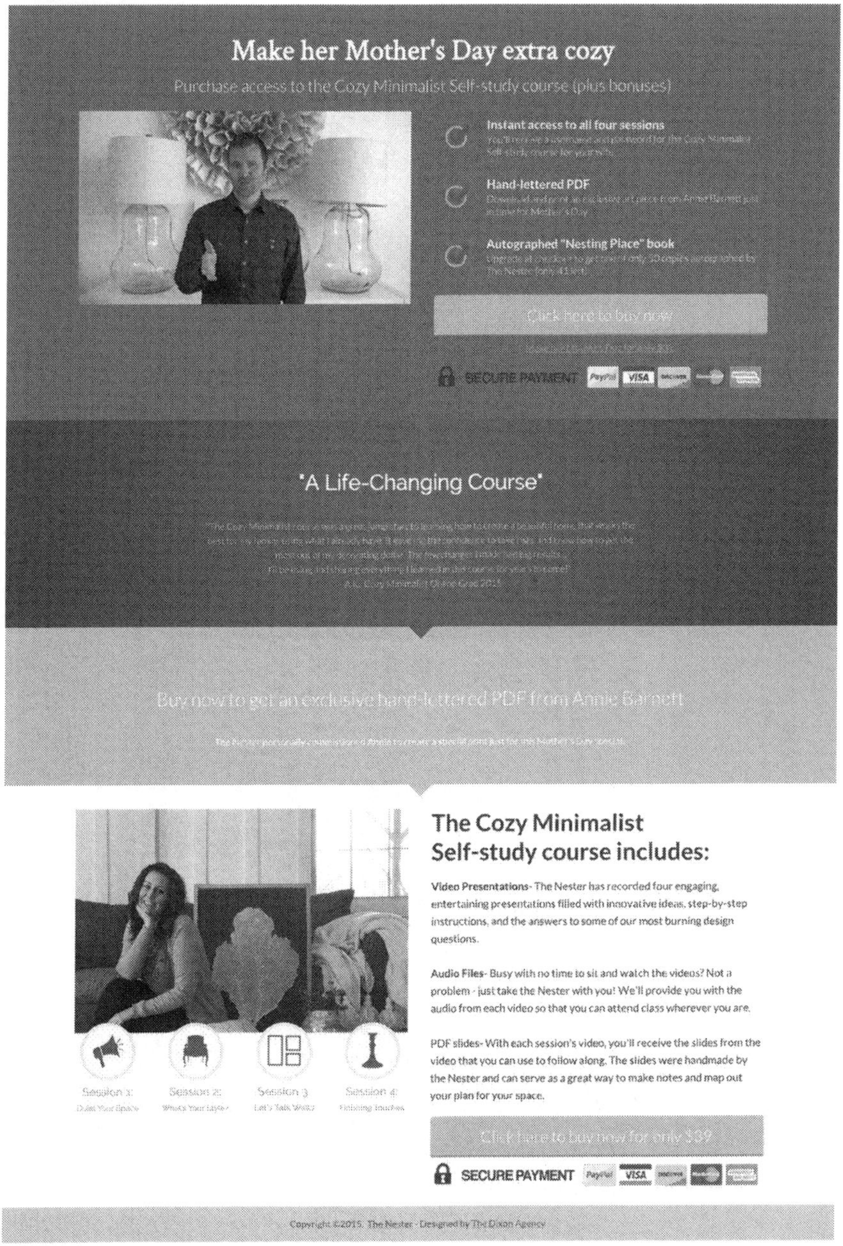

Sales page | 113

Figure 7: This sales page was created for a Mother's Day special for The Nester's Cozy Minimalist Self-study course. I featured a fun video and clear features and benefits.

Outline of the program

The second most important element of your sales page, besides an overview video, is an outline of the program. Even if you have a hot list of prospects who are willing to throw money at you no matter what you have to offer, it's still important to tell them what they're getting for their money. Outlining the program can help them make the decision that much easier.

For example, one of our clients has a three-week coaching program for practicing attorneys who want to start their own practice. On the sales page he outlines what content will be covered over each of the three weeks. Week one covers this topic, two covers this topic, and week three covers this topic.

In addition to the content of the program, you will also want to include the delivery mechanism. How do people access the content? What format is it available in? Are they slides, videos, audio downloads, transcripts?

Will people have to call in live? Will people have access to a discussion board or another way to submit a question?

There are many delivery details you can share, but again, you're looking for that balance. Don't overwhelm your customer - when in doubt, keep it in. Remember, you're trying to convince people to give you money; it doesn't hurt to explain what they're going to get for that money.

Testimonials

Testimonials are short statements of proof that your program works from previous customers. I recommend testimonials that are short with an attached color photo of that former customer. Include two or three testimonials at least.

Features and Benefits

Include both features and benefits. A rookie mistake is when only one is included. Features are the highlights of the program. What the program will include such as how it's delivered, what content will be covered, and how people access the content. Benefits are why your customer should care.

Figure 8: We created this sales page for Jeff Yalden's Teen Suicide Prevention Webinar. It featured a compelling video Call to Action and an overview of the features and benefits.

Clear results

Your sales page should include the clear results that people can expect to get once they join your program. No matter what you have to offer there is something people will get as a result of going through your program. For example they will learn, discover, understand, be able to, gain, lose, etc.

Make it clear to your potential customers what they will get by becoming customers. "By going through my program you can expect to…" - this is what your customer is buying. They want to receive results, and they're willing to trade their money and time for your teaching in order to receive your results. This is why testimonials make such a big difference because you can speak specifically to someone else's results.

A quick note: there are ever-changing rules from the FCC, the Federal Communications Corporation, about what you can promise and what you can sell online. Always be sure that your sales page includes the right disclaimer to avoid breaking any laws. One way to make sure your sales page covers everything it needs to is to benchmark your sales page against three other sales pages of gurus in your industry. They have likely done their research and have the right disclaimer(s) in order to comply with federal guidelines. To be extra safe, it would be a great idea to consult an attorney who can advise you on the latest changes in the law. Please remember that I am not an attorney nor do I play one on the Internet, so nothing in this book should be taken as legal advice. You should always consult with a professional.

Clear content

It is important for your sales page to explain exactly what is covered in your online course or within your product. What are the contents? What topics are covered in this course? How is the content broken down into modules? Be sure to reframe the content for the benefit of the potential customer. For example if you have an advanced training module, explain how this advanced training module is for people who have mastered the other concepts within the course.

Guarantee

I also recommend that you always offer a 100% moneyback guarantee. This is standard practice and is nothing special but without it, people will feel like they are taking too big a gamble. There are those who have played with a more than 100% guarantee such as double your money back, full refund, but keep the free bonus, and more. These all seem a bit gimmicky to me and distract from the purpose of the program. When your program is good all you need to do is say, "If for any reason you are not 100% satisfied with this program, contact us for a full money back refund." Websites usually include a nice little graphic of a gold ribbon seal with the number 100%.

Clear audience

When someone visits your sales page, it should be clear whether or not they are the right audience for your product. A phrase I love and use often is, "This program is for you if... ." You might also say, "This program is not for you if... ." For example, with Parker, "This program is for you if you are frustrated with making cold calls. You are willing to do the work but know that there is a better way." Another quote could be, "This program is not for you if you are looking for a quick fix or a lazy solution or are trying to scam or trick your customers."

Clear value

Value should be equivalent to 10 times the price. Think about the life change someone will experience as a result of going through your course. Will they make more money? Will they save more time? Will they finally have a breakthrough that they've been struggling with for years? Put a dollar value on that and the results. For example, if they will increase their sales by $1,000 on average in the first three months after going through the program, it is reasonable that you could charge $100 for the program. If they could increase their salary by $5,000, then it is reasonable that you could charge $497 for your program. The price should be 1/10 of the perceived value. Perceived value is understood in the mind of your customer, not something you just made up. I really hate seeing sales pages where they include a bonus transcript of an interview and say it has a $10,000 value. That is absolutely ludicrous. A transcript of an interview really has no value except for what you're going to learn from that transcript. When in doubt, price low because you can always raise your prices later.

Clear offer

The sales page is the primary place where you will explain exactly what you are offering. A sale is a basic exchange: you give me this and I give you this. Sales pages that don't convert are not clear in what they are offering. What exactly is being included? What will I get when I give you my money? Before we talk about the value, you have to explain the contents. For example, if you are hosting an online training course, what do the students actually get? A very clear answer follows:

- 9 10-minute videos for over 90 minutes of video training
- Audio versions of these videos
- Transcripts text based versions of these videos

One element of the sales page that is frequently missing is a clear offer. In fact, this is the most important part of the sales pitch. Essentially, a clear offer includes, "Here is what you get, here is what you pay." You should be able to summarize a clear offer in just one sentence.

Complete the following exercise.
"For only X, you will receive X!"
That's it. It's not going to get clearer than that.

- "For only $47, you will receive access to my six week course to help you create quote pictures for your social media profiles."
- "For only $97, you will receive instant access to my online video blog academy with 37 training videos, access to our private Facebook group, and downloadable templates you can use to improve your business related videos."

A clear offer includes the price and what the customer will receive.

Call to action

Any good sales page, really any website at all, should have a call to action. This is where you explicitly tell someone what they should do next. Common calls to action include "click here," "click the Buy Now button," "click the button below to get started," "add your name and email," "click download to get our free PDF checklist."

Calls to action are what drive traffic on the Internet. You need to make your website, your sales funnel, and especially your sales page, a step-by-step process. With each step along the way, your visitor is gaining momentum, and as long as he/she is guided in a logical direction using basic tools of human psychology, you can help lead a visitor to become a subscriber to become a customer.

Figure 9: We created this short sales page for the monthly membership site Hope*ologie to allow current members to log-in and prospects to learn more all on one page.

How to create a sales video

Using your laptop, write your script on your computer screen. Read the first bullet point out loud and look at the web camera on the computer and explain the first bullet point. Finish the sentence with your eyes locked on the web camera, then look down, read the next bullet point, look back up at the web camera and talk about the next bullet point. Continue this until you have covered all of the content necessary for your online sale. Once you've finished, put this video into a video editing program such as iMovie or Windows Movie Maker, and simply delete each of the sections where you look down at your scripts.

This isn't complicated, and it is something you can do today.

Now, each of these elements can be improved. For example, you could use a video camera instead of your computer's camera, you could use a microphone such as a snowball or a lapel microphone to improve the audio quality of your video, you could hang a sheet or a curtain behind you to make it look like you recorded your video in a studio, and you can add a logo and music to your video to add extra production value.

Whatever you choose, remember the purpose is to finish your online sales video so that you can make sales.

Expert tip

If you really want to take your video to the next level, allow me to paint a picture of what your video could look like. I share this vision not to overwhelm you, but to inspire you as to what is possible.

Tell the story. Your customers are facing a problem. A problem that is solved by your products. Allow the beginning of your video to tell the story of the pain your customers are experiencing.

Introduce the search. Show that your customers have been looking for an answer, that they've been trying to find a way to solve the problem, and nothing has worked.

Then, introduce the hero. The hero is the underdog, the researcher, and the hero is actually a customer. The hero had the same problem, was struggling in the same way, but instead of giving up she discovered the answer.

Introduce the "what" of the answer. Describe what is needed to solve the problem and explain how it works. Then compare your solution to all the other solutions that are out there. Explain how your solution is faster, cheaper, more intuitive, simpler, easier to understand, more efficient, or less hassle than any of the other products or programs available elsewhere. Then introduce value. Talk about how much a solution like this would cost and should cost. Finally, explain the convenience of purchasing and introduce a call to action.

To take it to the next level, you can even introduce a few client testimonials and, if possible, have them on video explaining their positive experience.

Is this sounding like an infomercial yet? Chances are it is, and the reason it sounds like an infomercial is because those formats work. That's it, they work! So, if possible, create a sales video that engages your audience and converts them from subscribers to customers.

Video hosting options

There are many options to choose from when it comes to hosting your sales video online. The best options are:

- YouTube- free, but may include advertising
- Vimeo- low monthly fee, no advertising
- Wistia- larger monthly fee, includes advanced features

Advanced features for video hosting:

As you consider the service to use for your video hosting, here are a few advanced features to help take your business to the next level:

- Analytics - learn what percentage of your video has been watched to find out where people stop viewing.

- Annotations- include visual calls to action in your videos. For example, you could say, "Click here to download my free PDF."
- Opt-in box - with this feature (sometimes called "turnstile"), you can require viewers to enter their email before finishing the video.

Pricing Strategy

So, how much do you charge? This is a question that a lot of beginners struggle with, and even some of the experts are still figuring out exactly the best way to price their products and programs.

There are those who recommend you do a market survey to figure out what others are charging and be competitive with them. You might purposely position yourself as more or less expensive, depending on whether or not you want to promote yourself as higher end or the perfect fit for a budget conscious consumer.

Marie Forleo explains that pricing is completely subjective and just has to do with your guts. How bold are you? That's it. Pricing has to do with your confidence.

I prefer a more systematic approach to pricing. Keep in mind these considerations:

- **Positioning**: Decide if you want your product to be a bargain or a stretch. You really can't do both. If you want your product to be a stretch, then you should price it at what is reasonable, plus a percentage.
- **Value**: People will pay what you charge if it is worth it to them. If they feel that they will get a good return on their investment, then they will buy. I have been amazed at both the high-end and low ball offers I've been seeing online recently. An eight week course can easily sell for $2000, and a six week course can sell for $39. Pricing online is very subjective.
- **Demand**: Is there sufficient demand for your product or program? Build up a conversation in the mind of your end user. Build a

promotional campaign, a great lead magnet with an autoresponder campaign and you can help increase demand for your product-which may allow you to charge more.

Price is a secondary consideration

You've likely seen the long-form sales page which, when scrolling down, can reach several pages in length. The typical response to one of these pages is to scroll and scroll and scroll until you get to the bottom and see the price and make a decision based on price. But price should never be the primary consideration for your customers.

Instead, you should offer value. What is the value someone's going to receive as a result of your product or program? This should be in stark contrast to the price. If they believe that they're going to get $10,000 worth of value from your product or program, then you can price it all the way up to $1000. Now you might not charge $1000, but it would be reasonable that you would charge 1/10 of the results that your customers will receive from your program.

NEXT STEPS

Best Practices

Now that you have a clear framework for growing your impact and income online, here are a few best practices we have developed with our clients over the last few years that could benefit you.

Establish measurable benchmarks.

How do you know if your platform is growing? The easy answer is you don't; unless you are measuring. The great thing about your website is that it is fairly easy to get a basic measure of how you are doing.

I recommend measuring the following:

- **Impact** - this is the number of people with whom you are communicating. These can be measured in visitors, subscribers, and customers. It's important to know these three numbers and to focus your efforts on growing the three numbers.

- **Income** - a second category I look at is income, otherwise known as sales. You should have a few products that you're able to sell and track the sales data for each. If you were just starting off, these products might be affiliate products where you get a commission percentage of every sale that is generated when someone clicks one of your links.

  I also highly encourage you to create your own products. For example, you can create a low-priced online course or a coaching program. Think about what you know and how that would benefit your ideal audience. Even if you created a three week course which featured three weekly live phone calls, some video training, and downloadable audio and video; you could charge a few hundred dollars. Imagine the feeling when you receive a PayPal alert on your phone telling you that you made a sale for $200. It happens to me daily and I still get excited. I love the feeling of knowing that I'm helping someone and supporting my family and growing my business every time one of my clients sells one of their products or programs.

Relaunching

Relaunching to your list once you make that first impression, you can repeat the first five of the six steps of the online sales formula over and over again. All you need to use is FLOATS: A lead magnet that is attractive to your email subscribers, followed by an opt-in page, followed by an autoresponder campaign, teasing the offer through your emails, and finally making the sale.

Launching a re-engagement campaign

What if you already have a list?

What if you have a list that's old?

Is it possible to re-engage your list?

A few months ago, I actually had a question for one of our clients. This particular client uses Constant Contact, an email marketing program that we do not recommend, and had not emailed his list for five months. We wondered if it would be possible to re-engage his subscribers, even though so much time had passed since the client had last written to them.

A general rule to follow for email frequency is that your list should hear from you at least once every 3 to 8 days. When more than a week and a half goes by between communications, your list loses interest in hearing from you and they begin to unsubscribe.

But this client hadn't emailed his list for almost 6 months. As far as we were concerned, it was like he didn't have an email list at all. But then we applied FLOATS to his list and something surprising happened.

We created an email with the same tone as a Facebook ad. In fact, we treated the email like a Facebook ad. It was highly targeted, it was actionable, it was timely, and it had a valuable lead magnet.

One nice thing about using email to re-engage your list, is that you have control of the subject line. Email is still the most personal medium on your computer. Everyone checks their email. It is a private place.

So, if you have people's email addresses, even if you haven't mailed them for a year or more, don't give up on that list. We engaged them using the FLOATS model. I looked at this client's former emails and realized that they lacked an updated design, so that was the first thing we focused on. We Photoshopped a nice custom header for the email and included a graphic for the downloadable lead magnet. The copy was tight and to the point.

We sent it out in December, which is a time that most people begin to think about the new year, so the focus of the email was all about planning the next year. Even though it had been a while since he emailed his list and engaged them through email, as we expected, he still came from a credible place.

Here's what we saw:

- an open rate of 74% percent
- a click through rate of 43% percent
- for those who opted in, we saw 6% go on to purchase the $40 upsell.

Bear in mind, all of this data is only within the first 24 hours. My philosophy on email is, if they don't take action on it in the first 12 hours, they might as well have deleted it.

Many clients we work with have some sort of an email list. Now it might only be 30 or 40 or 50 people on the list, but these are people who have raised their hand and said, "I want to learn more from you."

How do you reengage your list?

So what's the process for re-engaging? Simply craft an email that serves as an introduction. Treat this as an opportunity to give away a lead magnet in exchange for a re-engagement.

We use a re-engagement campaign to help move a list over from one system to another. For example, one of our clients currently uses Mail Chimp and has over 40,000 subscribers. We moved him over to Ontraport, our favorite email marketing tool, and crafted a real engagement campaign with a free video series. By opting into the free video series, these customers were raising their hands and re-engaging in the brand. We were able to learn who is still interested, and it helped us refresh the contact list.

The second email subject line is:

"In case you missed it, (first name)…"

This is a chance to engage people who didn't click on the original email. Even using an inferior email marketing program like Constant Contact, you can send an email to people who didn't click and opt in to the original re-engagements email.

Be conscientious of your email list and their reading patterns. You may feel you have a stronger list that can handle multiple emails, or it may be better for you to focus on people who haven't opened any correspondence from you period. With that group, I use "last chance" in the subject line. People read emails that have the subject line "last chance" because they don't want to be left out. It may be that they're procrastinating, so this is truly the last chance for them to engage. After that, you can focus on your new list of people who are re-engaged. No sense wasting your time with people who aren't going to take action.

Your monthly marketing plan

FLOATS begins with a monthly marketing plan divided into two week long campaigns every first and third Monday. As an example, your list will receive an email offering a free download.

All they need to do is click on the link in the email which will take them to an opt in page.

Once a subscriber has opted in to the free download, send the following sequence

Email 1: Here is your free PDF

Email 2: An Advanced Tip + Teasing the Offer

Email 3: A Testimonial

Email 4: Hard Sale

That's it; no more email after that

It ends up being five emails total. One to your entire list offering the free download, and then the four emails. I work through the sequential sequence.

You'll see the FLOATS formula at work frequently, if you follow any of 'today's top online marketers.' The reality is the list needs to be nurtured. You can't just constantly sell to people on your email list unless that's their expectation. Instead, offering something of value that stands on its own with a four email nurturing sequence after the download is a smart idea.

It can be very tempting to send all five emails to your entire list. But I recommend against that. If your list, besides the subscriber list, decides not to opt into the free download, they have indicated that they are not interested in that kind of offering. Why would you then spend the next four emails harassing them about something they're not interested in? It's the equivalent of someone at a fast food restaurant bringing you fries more than once. "Are you sure you don't want fries. Maybe you'd like to supersize your fries. We also have curly fries. Have we mentioned our french-fry-flavored fries?" I'm annoyed just writing those lines, let alone having to hear them or read them in an email sequence. Make the offer once and move on.

Using business intelligence

One of the main reasons to use a more advanced program such as InfusionSoft or Ontraport is because it will let you know a lot more about your customers' behavior. You can see when they've visited your site, which emails they've open, what they've clicked, and what they purchased. When you know how your audience engages, you can improve your marketing to better serve your customers.

ADVANCED TECHNIQUES

If you have been marketing online for more than a few years, you may want to check out some of the tips in this section. But be fairly warned, some of the ideas in this section are just ideas - not fully fleshed out. So, proceed with caution, but just a warning - some of this may be above your head (if you are just starting out).

Website Analytics

Google Analytics is a free tool to super-power your website. By installing Google Analytics, you can know almost anything you want about the people who visit your site, what they do while they are there, where they come from, how long they stay, and when they leave. In fact, Google Analytics is your most powerful tool for improving your website - because there is so much you can learn from this powerful tool.

Here are a few tips we have learned about Google Analytics:

1. Discover your most popular pages and posts (I then reshare these on social media using meetedgar.com)

2. Set up a goal to track sales
3. Create a custom audience to set you up for online advertising when you do launch your first product

Autoresponders based on user behavior

If you are using an advanced CRM (such as Ontraport, Salesforce, or InfusionSoft), you can fire off sequences based on user behavior (for example, when someone visits a certain website or orders a particular product). So even though a standard autoresponder sequence would have five emails that are general topics, when someone indicates an interest in a specific topic, they're led down a different funnel, but either way, the entire funnel is helping to educate the subscriber into becoming a customer.

The coolest thing about sending an email is that you can track the behavior and actions people take on that email. You can then fire off sequences based on what they do. For example, you can see if you bought opens, clicked or downloaded. If someone hasn't taken action on the first email, it doesn't make sense to have the second one fire off. This is an advanced tip and something we can help you with at the Dixon Agency.

Abandoned Cart

Abandoned cart is when someone begins to take action such as adding an item to the shopping cart on Amazon and then never completes the transaction. This also happens when someone clicks to download your lead magnet. Something about the process or something in their own life distracts them from completing the action. In fact, it is this transaction that will make all the difference between you building a robust subscriber list, which can be converted into customers, and you spending a lot of time and money on brand-new sites and Facebook ads and never seeing any results.

Retargeting

Once someone has visited your site they have to raise his/her hand to say he/she might be interested in what you have to offer. Now let's talk about what would happen if they do not respond or if they actually decline.

Once someone comes to your site they have the option to opt in to your lead magnet by entering their name and email or not opt in. But the good news is this is not the end of your engagement with them. If they decide to move on and never visit your site again, there is still a way for you to share your information on their screen, no matter where they go online.

Introducing Retargeting

Retargeting is an advertising strategy used on Facebook and the Google display network. Here's how retargeting works: let's use Parker as an example. Parker has created a downloadable file of five sales scripts that have been proven to increase sales. He's currently running a Facebook ad to offer this opt-in as a free lead magnet to get people into his sales funnel and to eventually have them sign up for his $500 online course teaching independent sales professionals proven sales strategies.

When someone clicks his Facebook ad, they land on a customized page focused on having them opt in to the lead magnet. But there is a percentage of people who land on the page and do not convert or actually enter their name and email address to download the five free sales scripts.

There are a few possible reasons for this:

- They got busy
- They weren't interested in the sales scripts
- They need to be warmed up before they're willing to trade their name and email for something Parker had to offer
- They don't trust Parker yet

Most of these objections can be overcome through an advertising strategy known as retargeting. When someone visits the site, there is a pixel that is loaded on their computer from Parker's site. This pixel is saved on the computer, indicating that the computer has visited Parker's site. Parker then creates a second ad offering a different lead magnet, such as a sales call worksheet PDF for free, and tells Facebook to only run that ad to people who have the pixel on their computer. This is known as a secondary audience.

The first audience is comprised of the people Parker targeted with that first ad on Facebook. The secondary audience is composed of people who have clicked the ad and visited Parker's website. The coolest thing about retargeting is that there are unlimited audience opportunities.

You could then create a third audience for people who downloaded the sales scripts, a fourth audience for people who visited the sales page for Parker's online course but didn't buy, a fifth audience for people who click the Add To Cart button for Parker's course but didn't buy, and a sixth audience for people who bought Parker's course and viewed the thank you page including an upsell offer for personal coaching.

Each of these audiences can be seen as part of a continual stream moving from low commitment to high commitment and moving from low interest to high interest.

The amazing thing about retargeting is that you can set goals and track return on investment. For example, you can determine that someone who has opted into your lead magnet but not purchased your course is three times more valuable than someone in your first audience that you were targeting but hasn't clicked your ad.

What about the user's perspective?

If you've used the Internet in the last year or so you have been retargeted. Most major websites that you go to use retargeting. You see it on the banner ads on news sites such as CNN, on the sidebar of sports websites such as ESPN, and all across social media including Facebook and even your Google searches. Each of these websites that you visit is placing a pixel onto your computer that's being used to define the audience to advertise to.

When you think about it, it's actually pretty genius. Instead of a large restaurant chain trying to target everybody they're only advertising to people who have already gone to their website. This, in theory, indicates that you are somewhat interested in their food and what they have to offer because you went to their website.

As a side note, it's pretty hilarious when someone uses your computer that has different interests than you. You'll begin seeing retargeting ads for products and programs that you are not interested in.

For example, if my wife were to use my computer I would start to see ads on Facebook for homeschool curriculum, women's fashion, and beauty products. If I were to use her computer, she would begin to see ads for online marketing tools. Retargeting is becoming more common and can lead to some strange online experiences when a different user on your computer is being targeted with display advertising.

Sequences and Tags

Think about it: you are a professional - you make a living through sharing your message online. Don't you want the professionals in your life to use professional tools? Anybody who you work with should be using the best tools possible to get the job done. The dentist, the doctor, the carpenter, the plumber. And you, the content creator, should be using the best tools that are out there.

I'm constantly surprised at content creators, authors, speakers, and bloggers who are penny wise and pound foolish. They will waste so much time trying to get systems to work together that weren't meant to. They'll spend countless hours looking for workarounds when the easiest solution is just to upgrade their systems.

Maybe you fit into that category. Maybe you need to upgrade your systems. In order to truly and effectively utilize the FLOATS model it's important to be able to use tags and sequences. If your system does not allow you to tag a contact with multiple tags and to put contacts through a sequence based on their behavior, then you need to upgrade your systems.

Without these two features it will be difficult for you to have a successful online business that is truly maximized. I say truly maximized, because no matter how big or small your list is, you want to receive the highest level of revenue possible. You've likely heard the expression "money on the table."

Money on the table is when you have an audience who is ready to buy and you're not making any offers.

Several years ago, before I started the agency, I attended a conference in Nashville, Tennessee. The conference was awesome, and everyone left inspired and motivated to take action. And that last 20 minutes, after the standing ovation, when the expert got back on the stage to thank everybody for attending, I was expecting a pitch. In fact, there should have been a pitch. It's the best place for it. The customers are satisfied, they're motivated, and they're excited. At that point they are ready to buy.

People were ready to take their money out and buy whatever the conference host offered. It was the perfect opportunity to offer ongoing coaching or an online program or a certification program or some sort of follow up. Instead there was no offer at all. Not even a T-shirt.

I wrote this best-selling author an email and recommended that he not leave money on the table. He graciously wrote me back and explained that that just isn't part of his organization, that he felt that it was somehow slimy or sleazy to make an offer at the end of the conference.

As you might imagine, I vehemently disagreed with him because I wanted to give him money! I wanted to give him money because he had just changed my life! The conference was only a couple hundred dollars to attend, the flight was only a couple hundred dollars, so the entire experience might have been only five or $600. And yet the value I received was much more. I wanted to reciprocate. I wanted to say, "Thank you! Now, here's $100 for a coaching program or access to the online videos."

But instead I walked away with money burning a hole in my pocket. In the same way there are people on your email list right now who want to buy something from you. What you have to offer is very valuable for exactly where they are in life, and they are ready to take the next step. They need what you have to offer, and yet you're not making the offer.

Now, the response I received from people who are inexperienced in this industry is, "I don't have a good system," or, "I don't want to always try to sell people." But the answer is not that you're always trying to sell someone, the answer is that you really don't have a good system. Because a good system makes the offer when the buyer is ready.

For example, we just finished an email promotional campaign where the client offered a free downloadable checklist. For everyone who opted in to download the checklist, there was a simple upsell. The checklist was free; the toolkit was $40. Over 300 people downloaded the checklist, and 10 people bought the tool kit. 10 people. That's a 3% return. 3% of the people who got the free thing wanted to buy the next thing. If you think about it that way, 3% of your audience wants to buy, too. And as the saying goes, "people hate to be sold, but they love to buy." There were people, at least 10, who downloaded the free checklist and thought, "I really want to thank this person, and the best way I know how is to give them some money."

So are you allowing your audience to thank you? Take the time to figure out how you can make that possible. Just giving people the opportunity to buy something, that's really all they need. Because there are people in your tribe who want to buy as long as you give them the right opportunity. I'm not saying you should open up a 'Donate Now' button. I have always found those to be a bit conniving. Why would somebody donate when all you need to do is offer an upsell? It could be as simple as, hop on a call or join the coaching program. And the coaching program doesn't even have to be built out; it could simply be three coaching calls that are live group coaching, Thursday nights from 8 to 9 Eastern, three weeks for $300. That's $100 per session for people to change their lives. That's all we are talking about.

There are people in your tribe who want to take their knowledge to the next level and you have an opportunity to offer that to them. If you have a system that doesn't help you identify who these ideal candidates are based on their behavior, then you are leaving money on the table. You're missing opportunities for engagement. Opportunities to serve your ideal audience the way they want to be served. You don't need to offer thousands of new opportunities or a dozen new products; let's not go overboard. But I recommend three levels of products:

Low-priced, mid-priced, and high-priced.
A low-priced offer is between $20 and $99, a mid-priced offer is between $97 and $397, and a high-priced offer is $1000 plus. There are people in your tribe who want to pay you $1000 or more. Think about that - $1000! People want to pay you $1000! If you could just find 100 people to pay you $1000 somewhere over the course of the year, think about what that would do for your business.

That is the kind of opportunity you have by implementing a system with sequences and tags. So don't give up, take action! Upgrade your systems because your systems are worth it.

You've got this!

BONUSES

Three email sequence to sell self-study course

I created these three email sequence for The Nester when we launched the Self-Study version of her Cozy Minimalist Online Coaching Program. The subscribers were already very much aware of the program, but decided not to purchase either due to a relatively high price point for that market ($89), the timing of the live webinars (four Thursday mornings in March), or other reasons. The Self-Study course was their opportunity to access the same content without the live interaction. The price point was substantially lower ($39 instead of $89) and the sales of this version have been more than triple that of the original version.

Email 1: Introducing the Opportunity
Subject: Wow! that was fun.

Hi *Name*,

The first class of the <u>Cozy Minimalist Online Coaching Program</u> just ended a few weeks ago.

It was amazing to see the transformations in so many homes.

People even said the program was "life-changing" and "refreshing". Wow!

Now that the live program is over, I wanted to give you an early peek at our new <u>Self-study course</u>.

It's not interactive like the more expensive Online Program, but you'll see it is the perfect price for even very tight budgets!

Learn more and check it out here: <u>http://www.cozyminimalist.com/</u>

xo
Myquillyn

Email 2: Social Proof and Momentum
Subject: What a response!

Hey *Name*,

As you saw from my email yesterday, we just opened Cozy Minimalist Self-study Course.

For only $39, you'll get instant access to:

1. All four webinar video recordings
2. Downloadable audio of all four sessions to listen on the go
3. PDF slides of all four sessions.
4. Text version of the four weekly assignments

I would love you to be part of it, Name.

Click here to get Instant access: http://www.cozyminimalist.com/

xo

Myquillyn

Email 3: Straight Sale

Note: this email is the last one they receive in the sequence. If they don't buy based on this email, they probably will never buy. So this one is more focused on the straight sale. Here is the offer, take it or leave it. Just clarify the features and benefits and make the sale.

Subject: Don't you just love before and after pictures?

Hey *Name*,

If you haven't been over to the Nesting Place blog today, I just posted six of my favorite before-and-after pictures from students in the Cozy Minimalist program.

Although the live portion has come to an end, you can still get instant access to the course content in our Self-study option.

And best of all, it's only $39 for all four sessions.

Click here to get instant access: http://www.cozyminimalist.com/

I hope you can join us!

xo

Myquillyn

14 Income Channels

Another bonus I would like to offer you is my 14 income channels infographic. Here are 14 different types of products you can create based on one message.

Let's connect

Now is the time to get started. You can do this. If there is anything we can do to help, please check out DixonAgency.org. You'll find a list of all of our services to help you increase your impact and income online.